Praise for *Out to Sea*

"*Out to Sea* is a fascinating, practical book that not only provides insight but makes me feel ready for my child's next journey. Radi's stories, tips, and thoughtful suggestions just make sense! I highly recommend this book and look forward to her next masterpiece."

—Dr. Daniel Bittman, Superintendent, Sauk Rapids–Rice School District

"*Out to Sea* offers an in-depth view of what it's like to send your child to college. As a school counselor, I will definitely recommend it to parents of high school seniors for years to come."

—Noel Meyer, Licensed School Counselor

"A helpful read for a parent sending a student off to college. The analogies and practical tips are helpful and presented in a thoughtful checklist manner."

—Mike Connolly, Dean of Students, Saint John's University

"Transitioning your child to the collegiate world is an exciting and emotional time for all. *Out to Sea* gives personal, helpful insights to this experience. It helps you navigate this journey and allows you all a more successful transition. A good read for all parents starting this journey."

—Lori Reesor, Vice Provost for Student Affairs, Indiana University

OUT to SEA

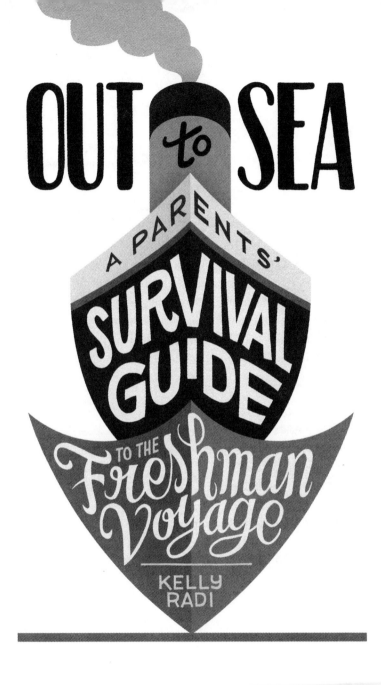

OUT to SEA

A PARENTS' SURVIVAL GUIDE TO THE Freshman Voyage

KELLY RADI

BEAVER'S
POND
PRESS

Cover art by Kevin Cannon
Edited by Angela Wiechmann
Photography by Kristie Anderson at KEA Photography

ISBN 13: 978-1-59298-726-9

Library of Congress Catalog Number: 2016911153

Printed in the United States of America
First Printing: 2016
20   19   18   17   16   5   4   3   2   1

Book design by James Monroe Design, LLC.

BEAVER'S
POND
PRESS

Beaver's Pond Press, Inc.
7108 Ohms Lane
Edina, MN 55439–2129
(952) 829-8818
www.BeaversPondPress.com

To Brooke and Karen
for the privilege of being your mom

Acknowledgments

Without the following people, this book would still be a "someday" idea brewing in my head. A heartfelt thank-you to each one of you who helped make this dream a reality:

- Marty, my biggest blessing and the love of my life—your unconditional support amazes me.

- Brooke and Karen, my inspiration and motivation— thanks for letting me share your stories.

- Alison, my heart-sister, biggest cheerleader, and sounding board.

- Becca, my calming voice of reason and trusted advisor.

- My parents, for preparing me to sail.

Thanks also to the talented crew at Beaver's Pond Press:

- Lily and Hanna, for your ability to keep me moving full speed ahead.

- Angela, my brilliant editor and Queen of Transitions. The tiara is yours!

- Laurie, my marketing guru, for sharing your passion for Twitter.

- Alicia, for your red pen and sharp eye.

- Kevin and Jay—your talents never cease to amaze me.

Many thanks to the numerous people willing to share their stories and offer perspective, especially Laura, Carla, Candice, Beth, Lori, Gayle, Coke, Jean, Jody, Kristie, and Michelle.

Much gratitude to the many professionals who gave their time and expertise, including:

- Shelden Agbayani, California Lutheran University

- Dr. Sentwali Bakari, Drake University

- Dr. Kimberly Christensen, Sartell Pediatrics

- Michael Connolly, Saint John's University

- Department of Public Safety, Princeton University

- Dr. Marie Dick, St. Cloud State University

- Sr. Mara Faulkner, Order of St. Benedict

- Dr. Cara Halgren, University of North Dakota

- Nikki Heyd, Kappa Alpha Theta

- Dr. Kaarin Johnston, College of St. Benedict and St. John's University

- Scott Law, Drake University

- Chancellor William McRaven, The University of Texas System

- Dr. Troy Payne, CentraCare Health Sleep Disorders

ACKNOWLEDGMENTS

- Dr. Lori Reesor, Indiana University

- Meredith Rogers, St. Cloud State University

- Dr. Melissa Sturm-Smith, Drake University

- Jody Terhaar, College of St. Benedict

- Dr. Janet Tilstra, St. Cloud State University

And finally, a great big thank-you to the many college students, RAs, and recent graduates across the nation—especially Kylee, Rachael, Hadley, Jenna, and Jack—who humored me (the lady in mom jeans) in your student unions, coffee shops, and dorm rooms. It was a privilege to meet you and learn from you. The future is bright with you at the helm!

My heart overflows.
Thank you.
Kelly

CONTENTS

Introduction / 1

PART ONE
PREPARING TO SET SAIL

PART TWO
ANCHORS AWEIGH

PART THREE
BACK IN PORT

PART FOUR
REFLECTING ON THE VOYAGE

APPENDIX A
Words of Affirmation / *241*

APPENDIX B
Quotes to Inspire and Motivate / *243*

APPENDIX C
Care Package Ideas / *247*

About the Author / *257*

INTRODUCTION

Letting Go

I gripped his hand as if it were my lifeline. Terrified, I forced one hesitant foot in front of the other as tears rolled down my face. His strong hold was the only thing preventing me from throwing myself down on the pavement. Fighting the urge to turn around and sprint back to the source of this intense pain—all five feet three inches of her—I pushed forward toward our car in the dormitory parking lot.

Every fiber of my being wanted to run back into the brick building and up the three flights of stairs just to squeeze one more precious hug out of our firstborn. To the world, she was a polished, articulate young woman. But to me, she was still my baby.

After all, I was the one who birthed her, changed her diapers, and taught her how to pump her legs on the swing. I led her Girl Scout troop and taught her how to apply mascara. I held her, all puffy eyed and broken hearted, after her first breakup (secretly glad the "relationship" was over). And I was the one who snapped her picture when her college acceptance letter arrived and set this whole thing in motion.

From the day that letter arrived, I was a mess—a mixed bag of conflicting emotions. I was excited for my baby to embark on this new adventure. I was also terrified to let her go. Fear-induced questions flooded me in waves. Would she be safe? How could I protect her with 321 miles between us? Would she make nice friends? Would she get enough to eat? Would she advocate for herself if she struggled in a class? Would she know not to eat the fruit floating in the punch? Heaven forbid, if the situation came up, would she practice safe sex? Would she remember to call me—*not* about the sex, but just to check in once in a while?

Why was it so difficult to let her go? After eighteen years of pouring my heart and soul into raising this young human, how could I just plop her down on a college campus, walk away, and expect her to survive? The bigger question lurking underneath the surface was obvious: How would *I* survive?

I left a piece of my heart in Des Moines that day. Our somber five-hour drive home provided plenty of time to process what we, Brooke's parents, had just done. We were cruising north on I-35, doing our best to reconcile the conflicting emotions of anticipation and anxiety. I snorted and sobbed for the first hour of the trip.

My dear heartbroken husband, her daddy, sat silently with pursed lips, fighting back his own bittersweet tears. When you blend joy with pride and love and fear, that is what you get. Bittersweet tears.

Flashbacks of her childhood brought new waves of tears. Her premature birth—she was so helpless and tiny. Her perfectly bald head—she was nearly two before her fine blonde hairs required cutting. Her shaky first steps in her tiny pink sneakers. Her Elmo-themed birthday party. Her little pink cast when she broke her foot for the first time. Her purple cast when she broke it the second time. Her reusable black Aircast for her third, fourth, and fifth breaks. (It's complicated, but let's just say she has "structural issues.") Her first jazz band solo and the profound joy making music brought her. Her first prom—elegant, radiant, and with a midnight curfew. Her high school graduation. And now, her first (gulp!) day of college.

I should have seen this reaction coming. The day before, I had started my morning as usual: I sat a too-hot-to-drink cup of coffee on the counter beside me and opened Facebook for my daily dose of social media. Up popped a photo of a beautiful blue-eyed girl in a Bethel sweatshirt, posing (no doubt to appease her mother) on her color-coordinated comforter atop her twin extra-long bed. Her freshly decorated dorm room reflected anticipation and new beginnings, but her smile revealed equal parts excitement and anxiety.

Tears pooled in my still-sleepy eyes before I could take my first sip. I knew this girl. She was my friend's daughter, her firstborn. Accompanying this photo, naturally, was a sorrowful post from her mother about letting go. It plucked at my maternal heartstrings like a melancholy guitar solo. I knew I was next.

Other parents—those who had already paddled down this rapid-filled river of letting go—posted heartfelt comments on my friend's Facebook wall. They offered support, comfort, and even humor. Like a thirsty sponge, I soaked up their wisdom, hoping it would provide me strength as I moved my own daughter the next day.

Their comments ran the gamut of "Best wishes to your sweet daughter" and "Thinking of you as you let go" to "Now you can rent out her room . . . for cash!" Another found a silver lining with "Try to think of it as less laundry to fold. #youwillsurvive." One emotionally charged mom sent an eloquent reminder that we are to help our children grow roots as well as wings.

And then our move-in day came. That morning, I had so many things I wanted to tell Brooke, but I couldn't seem to muster the words. So I took out a piece of paper and let my dreams for her flow from my heart (and brain) to my pen. It wasn't eloquent, but it was sincere. I share this letter at the end of the book.

Writing the letter gave me hope, closure, and a sense of purpose. I prayed reading it would give her courage, humility, and a sense of security. I later learned it calmed some of her fears, sooth-ing her on her first night in the dorm—her new home. The simple letter was the beginning of our new normal. A normal that would bring less mothering and more mentoring. Less hovering and more empowering. We had given her a safe harbor. Now we had to release her and let her hoist her sails.

There in the car, my blubbering eventually turned to sniffles, then to a quiet calm. Some of the bitter went away and left room for the sweet. I knew she was where she wanted to be, eager to test new waters and meet new people. I knew I had to cut the proverbial umbilical cord and hand my baby the oars to her own boat. With all the love and support I could muster, I had to send her out to conquer the wide-open sea.

But how could I do that? Where was the survival guide—the owner's manual—for parents of freshmen? I longed for a guide to help me navigate the unfamiliar route.

This true story, my fellow parents, is the inspiration for this book. I am not a psychologist nor a dean of students. I am not a professor nor a cruise ship captain. I am a real-life mom who has traveled these sometimes stormy seas. I've learned a few things along the journey.

My goal is to be your first mate and share what I've learned as you embark on your own voyage. I hope to help you survive (and thrive) as your child sets sail into the collegiate ocean of opportunities.

What to Expect: College Edition

As I watched a little pink plus sign slowly reveal itself on a stick twenty-one years ago, I wondered how our lives were about to change. The first thing I did was tell my husband our thrilling news. The second was to buy a book called *What to Expect When You're Expecting.*

This book became my pregnancy survival guide. I referenced it daily, comforted by advice from experts and women who'd carried babies before I did. The book told me when our baby was the size of a grape and when it grew fingernails. The book taught me what to eat (or not eat) to help curb my morning sickness. It helped me map out a birthing plan and prepared me for the big event.

In the years that followed, I found how-to books for parenting toddlers and talking to teens. So as our daughter neared high school graduation, I found myself once again unsure about the future—wondering what to expect as we sent her off to college. I searched for answers, for a guidebook. I found books on ACT preparation, college finances, and admissions. Several books were geared for the students themselves. But what I wanted was an honest, heartfelt, informative book written for parents of first-year college students by someone who truly grasped the tsunami of emotions I was experiencing.

Out to Sea: A Parents' Survival Guide to the Freshman Voyage is my version of *What to Expect* for parents as their children enter the first year of college. It is not intended for students but for you— the parents who love them and want to help them thrive.

Parents, please consider this book your survival guide. It's designed to help you navigate through many aspects of college life: from how to get the most out of orientation sessions and money matters to campus safety and roommate relations. This easy-to-read, informative, and sometimes humorous guidebook is swimming with real examples, tips, and checklists, such as what to pack (and not pack) for the dorm.

We'll also go beyond the practical topics. We'll discuss letting go and control issues (a personal challenge of mine) as well as how to successfully adjust your course at home. You'll find advice on appropriate, effective means of communication, and I'll address your deep, nagging parental fears and concerns.

The chapters are divided into sections spanning the first-year timeline, from summer preparations after graduation to your child returning home a year later for summer break. The sections walk you step by step through the process.

That said, different readers will start this book at different times. Perhaps some of you reading right now are immersed in your child's senior year (or even earlier). Your goal may be to learn everything there is to know about the freshman voyage well before the ship-out date. And perhaps others of you are already several months into the freshman year. You may be looking for information about a specific issue you're currently facing. Whenever you begin reading and whatever information you seek, my hope is that *Out to Sea* provides helpful guidance when you need it most.

My Writing Journey for Your Journey

During the course of writing of this book, I spent many hours on college campuses, immersing myself in the current college culture. Yes, I was the old lady hanging out in student centers, the one wearing mom jeans to the coffee shops.

In my research, I had the pleasure of meeting passionate people from all aspects of university life. I interviewed professors and provosts, housing administrators and financial aid workers, counselors and safety officers.

I was blown away by how administrators and staff at campuses large and small supported this project. From California to New Jersey, these professionals invest their time and talents in not only educating our students but also keeping them safe, healthy, and on course during this voyage. They see students come in as frightened freshmen and leave as confident graduates equipped to face the challenges of the real world. They are the wind behind our students' sails.

In addition to the time I spent with professors, administrators, and staff, I had the great privilege of talking with students—lots of students! These bright, inspired young adults give me hope for the future. I can tell you, the next generation is articulate and sincere with strong ideals and even stronger opinions. The students I met supported the concept of this book, many asking if I'd send a completed copy to their parents. These students were happy to share their experiences and offer honest advice for parents of incoming freshmen. Throughout the chapters, you'll find some of the best research material I can share with you, straight from the mouths of these student experts.

And let's not forget the parents. This book simply wouldn't be possible without the valuable insight from parents who've already launched their students. They are the experienced crew members with firsthand knowledge of the challenges and joys that come along with the journey.

They were willing to tell me what worked and what didn't, what they did right and what they'd do differently if they had the chance to do it again. They offered suggestions and wisdom gleaned from actual life experiences. A special thanks to you—you know who you are—for sharing your stories.

Note: While I use real names and identities for the faculty, staff, and experts I interviewed, I have protected the identity of most of the students and parents. In the instances where I do use students' real names, I have received permission to do so.

A Word on Words

In this book, you'll notice some quirks and may question my choice of words. Please let me explain . . .

Freshmen vs. First-Year Students

One of the professors I interviewed brought to my attention her concerns about my use of the word *freshman*. She explained that because it has *man* in it, it could be deemed sexist and exclusive of women. She said the gender-neutral term *first-year student* would be more appropriate.

This has been a topic of discussion among university administrators across the nation. While some administrators and professors I met used *first-year student* in our conversations, others used *freshman*, as did the hundreds of students I had the privilege of meeting.

I've opted to use both terms. Please know I mean absolutely no disrespect when I use *freshman* in this book. I use it with respect and love for all first-year students—regardless of gender. I'm also a mom, so you'll hear me affectionately calling them *children* and (my favorite) *babies*. After all, no matter how old they get, they'll always be our babies!

He and She

You'll notice that I randomly alternate between the pronouns *he* and *she* when referencing our beloved students. Again, this is not intended to offend. While most scenarios could apply to both genders, I opted to randomly reference just one gender at a time. It makes for a much easier read. If I were to use *he or she* and *him or her* every time I needed a pronoun, the book would be seven hundred pages long!

Traditional vs. Nontraditional College Experiences

Today's young adults have a plethora of opportunities available to them. Every student takes a different path. Some live at home. Some attend technical colleges or trade schools. Some choose to take a gap year for the opportunity to learn from volunteering or traveling the world. For many, it's financially necessary to work full-time and attend classes part-time. Other young people enlist in our nation's military branches. (A great big thank-you to them for their service.)

Each path is as unique as the person who walks it. That being said, I had to choose my own path in writing this book. While many of the topics in the book are relevant to a variety of postsecondary paths, I geared it toward parents of students enrolling in traditional four-year college programs.

Please refer to this guide often as you embark on your child's freshman voyage. Let's set sail!

PART
ONE

PREPARING TO
SET SAIL

ANCHORS AND SAILS

To reach a port we must set sail—sail,
not tie at anchor—sail, not drift.
—FRANKLIN D. ROOSEVELT

If you're reading this, you have survived graduation and your child has been accepted into the U of his future. Congrats to both of you!

If you're one of the 3.4 million families preparing to send your student off to college for the first time, you've likely already started preparing the physical things. You probably bought a laptop, shower shoes, and a dorm-sized fridge as soon as the acceptance letter arrived. Maybe even sooner.

But what about the rest? What about the emotional preparations? Have you started those?

Each child starts college only once. This milestone is a big one. We parents get only one shot at this moment of letting go. No pressure, right?

What can you do to equip him for success? What can you do or say to help the launch go smoothly? How can you impart wisdom? How can you enable independence? Your brain quietly tells you to give space and let go, but your heart screams, "Hold on tight!"

"When our oldest daughter left this year for her first year at university, it brought out insecurities I never thought I would experience," explains Jim, a dad of three girls. "I believe my wife and I raised her to make sound decisions and evaluate the consequences of her actions. I know she's a smart girl and ready to go. But I find it a struggle to let go and trust in the process. As parents, our brains tell us one thing and our hearts another. We know intellectually that our children will stumble and fall and that we will be there for them. But emotionally, it can be a struggle."

Many chapters in this book will help you make physical and practical preparations in the weeks before your child goes to college. But before we get to all that, let's start the emotional preparations by talking about anchors and sails.

The Anchor Theory

One of the most intuitive people I know is my sister-in-law Alison. She's a relaxed earth mother who possesses a Zen-like calm, which suits her career choice very well. I call her a baby whisperer. Others recognize her as a professional childcare provider. In either case, she's the real deal in effective child-rearing—a modern-day Mary Poppins.

On any given day, you'll find nearly a dozen "littles" exuberantly romping around her house. Now, please understand—if I had a dozen kids traipsing around my house, I'd probably be found hiding in the closet with a bottle of cheap merlot. But not Alison. No sir. With a spirit of tranquility, she's in the middle of the madness, kissing boo-boos and encouraging the use of inside voices.

Alison's career has given her incredible insight into human

development. I witnessed this firsthand a few years ago when we were at my parents' house for Christmas. Her young children—my adorable nieces and nephew—were playing in the next room, so she and I seized the rare quiet moment to sit back on the sofa and chat. Occasionally, one of her kids would walk over and show her a toy or just touch her, then scamper back to the playroom. I noticed they didn't want or need anything in particular. They simply checked in with their mommy.

When I asked her about it, she gave me an uncomplicated explanation: "Sometimes kids just need to anchor." She said they need to connect with their source of security, then they can comfortably resume their activity. They anchor and move on.

Of course, we parents have done our best to provide anchors for our children: safe and loving homes, core values, and faith foundations. Anchors, like roots, are embedded in tradition, and they create a sense of belonging. They're the superglue holding a family together through the good and not-so-good times. They're the unconditional love that bonds us.

Do you think Alison's anchor theory is exclusive to seven-year-olds? I don't think so. I believe it applies to teenagers and budding adults as well. Occasionally, they too need to anchor. They simply need to touch base with their parents—a source of security—for reassurance, then they resume their activity.

Your child is preparing to leave for college, to take the voyage into adulthood. This is a time unlike any other when she needs the sense of security you provide. In the months before she leaves—and in the months she's away—be aware of her need to anchor. It may be as simple as a conversation about friends or a comment about a current event. It may be a short text message. If you're lucky, it might be a hug or an "I love you."

In these moments, she's not looking for advice or lectures or more rules. As a parent, your goal is to listen and be the silent, nonjudgmental anchor of support she craves as she learns to unfurl her own sails. Being that anchor is one of the first steps in your evolving relationship.

The Sail Theory

It may be easy to understand the anchor theory as our children approach college. Being an anchor makes sense. You've been doing it since the day he was born.

But then there's the sail theory—that we must now give our children freedom, independence, and wisdom. That's a lot more challenging for parents to process. Freedom to make mistakes? Independence without boundaries? Wisdom to (hopefully) know what to do with the freedom and independence? Yikes!

Independence was an ideal and even motivating concept when they were toddlers. We would yearn for them to function on their own for even just fifteen minutes so we could enjoy a little independence ourselves.

As our children grew, however, there was a sting to the idea. Before we knew it, our kids were scheduling sleepovers and going to summer camp. They were attending concerts with their friends and spending less time with us. They began searching for significance and dreaming of future goals—goals that didn't include us.

Once that college acceptance letter arrived, independence took on a whole new meaning. How do you establish boundaries when your child hits eighteen and thinks he knows it all? Is it possible to give controlled freedom? Is there such a thing as sails with training wheels? How is it we want our children to be independent yet we don't trust their judgment?

As a parent of a newly minted adult, you need a well-charted plan and the ability to know when to throw that plan overboard.

Sails enable movement and growth, yet they require flexibility as the winds change. And the winds likely will change—a lot—once your child is off to college.

Larry and Theresa saw their daughter Anne off to a large urban school. She had an apartment off-campus with a friend from their small hometown, and she was ready to pursue her dream of becoming a veterinarian. On the first day of winter break, they found her crying on the couch. As it turned out, Anne had done poorly in her classes, hated living in a big city, and regretted moving in with her friend.

She announced a complete 180: she wanted to transfer to a small school in a small town and become a teacher. To Larry and Theresa, these ideas seemed to come out of nowhere. But after some serious consideration and a lengthy family discussion, they decided to step back and trust Anne's judgment. After all, it was her life and her consequences. And they sensed that she truly felt it was the best decision for her future.

This stage is incredibly difficult for a control freak like me. Like Larry and Theresa, I've had to pick the battles I deemed necessary and choose to let other issues fall away. The wisdom of a sixteen-year-old helped me in this area.

It's Just Different

We had the privilege of hosting a foreign exchange student for an entire school year when our girls were still in high school. Pauline, our German daughter, brought new ideas and fresh perspective to our lives. She was our bubbling ray of sunshine with her adorable accent and zest for life. She impressed us with her courage and her openness to try new things. When faced with a foreign concept or new way of doing something, she would shrug her shoulders and say, "It's not right or wrong. It's just different."

What practical yet profound words from the mouth of a sixteen-year-old! This simple "it's just different" attitude is applicable in so many areas of life. Case in point, I spend too much time correcting the little things, such as how to load a dishwasher properly (i.e., *my* way), that I forget there are many other ways to accomplish this task.

The "it's just different" mind-set is especially relevant during this stage of burgeoning adulthood. Once they launch on their college voyage, our students will learn many—often unconventional—ways to accomplish tasks and solve problems. They likely won't do it the way we'd do it. But that's okay. We don't have to label it "right" or "wrong" as long as we recognize it as "different." Part of giving our children sails is letting them figure out solutions on their own and not judging the process.

Likewise, instead of judging others' parenting techniques, we should recognize that they're not right or wrong—they're just different. We come from different backgrounds and have different perspectives. We have different hot buttons. We pick different battles.

As parents, we each must set our own boundaries with our own children. Some of our techniques will work—some will not. There's merit to having an open mind and learning new techniques from other parents.

A Lesson in Ink

Now that we've discussed anchors, sails, and different strokes, let's talk tattoos. Of all things, tattoos provide a classic example of the emotional issues we parents face as our children ready themselves for this new voyage.

Young people today are sprucing up body parts with ink and adding holes to their heads (and elsewhere), all in the name of individuality and expression. Please understand—I have no issue with tattoos per se. In fact, I find many of them very beautiful, and I love the stories they tell (unless the story includes a fifth of Jack Daniel's and a dare).

That being said, I don't have a tattoo and have no plans to get inked in the near future. Call me old school. Actually, call me needle-phobic. For whatever reason, I have never had the urge to get one, not even back in the dark ages—when I was a new adult myself.

I recall a graphic arts class during my sophomore year of college. The professor was a middle-aged Birkenstocks-with-socks kind of a gal (again, not right or wrong—just different). She possessed some very strong opinions. This out-of-the-box thinker was determined to push her nontraditional views on our fresh, pliable, young minds. It was her way or the highway!

One day, she informed the class that it was our personal duty to express ourselves through body art (aka tattoos). After offering the class an intimate viewing of some of her own personal masterpieces, she delivered a rousing lecture on the subject and challenged us to create designs for our own future ink jobs.

She apparently saw the concern written all over my face. She called me out, asking if I had anything to share with the group.

With trepidation, I spoke up, the uneasy words trickling from my mouth. "Um, Professor, I was just thinking, um, that what seems like a good idea at nineteen might not seem like a great idea when you're old, um, like fifty." Feeling the need to clarify, I continued. "You know, what starts out as a rosebud here"—I pointed at my boob—"might grow into a long-stemmed rose over time."

Needless to say, I didn't do so well in that class.

Let's fast-forward a quarter century or so. One mother-daughter pair I know went out and got matching tattoos to commemorate the daughter's high school graduation. Female bonding via ink. A lifetime memento of the spring of 2014.

Instead of questioning her daughter's wishes, this mom chose to fully embrace them and head to the tattoo parlor too. She has no regrets. Her theory was, "If you can't beat 'em, join 'em."

Then there was our firstborn's eighteenth year. A year of freedom—when many of her peers were sneaking off to tattoo parlors. Her dad, a tattoo-free conservative, was no more thrilled than I about a lifetime reminder of our daughter's senior year imprinted on her ankle or boob or back—or anywhere else, for that matter. Brooke hadn't even mentioned tattoos, but with many of her friends getting inked, we wanted to be proactive. There are many different ways to raise children to be healthy, well-adjusted young adults (with or without body art). This was one battle we, as her parents, chose to fight.

While I tend to think with emotion, my darling hubby thinks like the businessman he is. So after a little research and some lively discussion between the two of us, we opted to take a businesslike approach in addressing potential body ink. We sat down to have a serious conversation with our still-tattoo-free daughter. We were armed with a stack of bills and a college fee statement.

We buttered her up by reiterating our parental pride in her accomplishments and acceptance into the college of her dreams. We affirmed our commitment to help her finance her education. Then we made it abundantly clear that as long as she was operating on our payroll, she simply could not afford a tattoo.

Call us control freaks. Call us old-fashioned. Call us parents. But it was true: We were bankrolling tuition, books, room and board. We were helping her with car payments, gas, and insurance. We were subsidizing her cell phone. Yes, she had a part-time job that paid pretty well. And yes, she did contribute. But her job did not afford her the luxury of ink.

Our opinion was that once she earns her degree, lands her first full-time job, and pays her own bills, then she can make the adult decision to purchase some permanent body art. (I only hope it's not a rosebud.)

Accustomed to her solid debating skills, we braced ourselves for her rebuttal. Imagine our shock when she said, "Okay. I get it. I didn't really want one anyway. What seems like a good idea now might not seem like a good idea when I'm old. You know, like forty."

Ouch.

A Safe Harbor

With these metaphors of anchors and sails, think of the college years as training for your new sailor. Your child has moved from the controlled dry docks of high school into the safe harbor of a university.

Being in the harbor brings new experiences and uncomfortable situations. But it also empowers our children with new communication tools and provides ample opportunities in which to learn to steer a vessel. Soon they will be confident enough to venture out at sea, in the open waters. For now, though, providing them with both anchors and sails is the best way we can support them and prepare them for the voyage ahead.

ARE YOU A
HELICOPTER PARENT?

*"I am not afraid of storms,
for I am learning how to sail my ship."*
—LOUISA MAY ALCOTT

As we discussed in chapter 1, it's best to spend less time judging and more time respecting different parenting styles. So let's move from anchors and sails to helicopters. Choppers. Whirlybirds.

As we continue to discuss the emotional aspects of your child entering college, helicopter parenting tops the list of parenting practices to be aware of during this time of transition. Again, this isn't about "right" or "wrong" or judging others. This discussion is designed to inspire us to review our own parenting practices and seek ways to improve how we interact with our children.

helicopter parent (noun, informal) a parent who takes an overprotective or excessive interest in the life of their child or children.

We parents are so concerned with our children's successes that we have conditioned ourselves to hover from the get-go. In an era of car seats, safety helmets, and cell phones, we are raising the most protected and programmed generation to date.

We begin with Baby Einstein at newborn play groups and morph into carefully monitored potty-training programs compete with charts and rewards. We give standing ovations for bowel movements. We spend hours planning and executing perfectly themed birthday parties. Forget clowns—they're so passé. I heard that one California mom hired a troupe from Cirque du Soleil to entertain her offspring!

As they "graduate" from preschool wearing tiny caps and gowns, we are already committing them (and our wallets) to specific athletic teams. Our elementary students, the free T-shirt generation, receive ribbons for participating at sport clinics and trophies for attending summer day camps. "Hey, Mom! Look at my trophy for coming in eleventh place! It's heavy. Can you help me carry it?" Parents line up like parade goers on soccer sidelines to critique practices and coaching skills.

What happened to the days where kids biked to T-ball and somehow made it home without any parental unit involved? Can you recall a time when there were no dads telling the coach how to coach and no moms waiting with coolers of rainbow-colored juice boxes and cases of organic protein bars? Kids were just kids. Sports were just for fun. Parents were just parents and didn't hover.

Raising kids in the '70s, my folks didn't have time to hover. They were busy with jobs and chores and the basics of child raising. They believed in teaching us to solve our own problems. If I was bored, I found a friend or read a book. My friends and I would pack our own lunches—bologna sandwiches on Wonder Bread—and pedal away on our bikes for a day of make-believe adventures at the local lake. We'd construct forts from fallen branches, play hide-and-seek on the island, and skip stones into the glistening water. We'd pretend we were pioneers on the prairie, living like Laura Ingalls, collecting pinecones and berries and poison ivy. We would play hard all day and return home sweaty, dirty, and in time for dinner. No organized teams. No scheduled craft time. No whistle-blowing officials wearing stripes. Absolutely no helicopter parents in sight.

Don't get me wrong. My parents were not absent. They, like most parents of that generation, just weren't hands-on 24-7. My mom might not have been a helicopter mom, but she sure did have radar ears and incredible intel. We were taught that actions had consequences. When I made a bad choice, I knew that whatever the public consequences were, my parental ones would be much greater.

Quiz: Are You a Helicopter Parent?

Still not sure if you're hovering too close? Take this quiz. At the end, add up your yes answers and check out your score.

1. Do you accompany your child to school functions looking like a personal pack mule with his backpack, instrument case, sports gear, and more?

2. Have you ever called a teacher or professor to challenge a grade she's "given" your child?

3. Do you call or text your child at least once every day?

4. Are you a human alarm clock for your child?

5. Do you fill out your child's paperwork at medical appointments?

6. Have you "helped" your child with a school project by doing 90 percent of the work?

7. Do you speak on behalf of your child when meeting with other adults?

8. Did you fill out your teen's college or scholarship applications?

5–8 yes answers

Yes, you are a helicopter parent. You hover. You "fix." While your intentions may be pure, you micromanage this young adult's life. Here's your opportunity to recognize you are actually hurting your child more than helping him. Understand your actions have long-standing consequences for your child's future—and not necessarily healthy ones. Think about it. If kids aren't challenged by a tough professor or caught in the act of making a mistake, how will they develop the resilience to thrive in the real world? How will your child learn the problem-solving skills to overcome obstacles? How will he grow the life skills necessary to thrive? But there's hope. *Now* is the time to shut down your chopper blades and empower him to become a life-ready adult. Take the first step and resist the urge to control. Put down your phone. Let him go and let him grow.

3–4 yes answers

You may not be hovering every single day, but your rotors are clearly on standby. Take a good look at your role and how involved you are in your student's life. You mean well and care deeply; however, you step in to help more often than necessary. If your intervention is needed to avoid a total disaster, of course you should act. But if your definition of "total disaster" is a bad grade or a roommate spat, you need to change your thinking. Always remember—mistakes can create powerful learning opportunities. Children grow and mature from these opportunities. By stepping back, you can instill confidence and independence. Practice asking,

"What are you doing to solve this problem?" The next time your child calls with a situation, you'll know how to react in a way that encourages her to find a solution. You are not a mechanic there to fix her issues. Rather, you can point her to her owner's manual to troubleshoot and correct them herself.

1–2 yes answers

You recognize the importance of enabling your child to solve problems on her own, but you still struggle with some boundaries. Most likely, you strive to do what is best for your child but catch yourself overparenting on occasion. Let this be an educational experience for both you and your child. All those things you're used to doing? Stop doing them. Soon your child will become the independent adult you've always dreamed of. At this time in your child's life, your job is to enable her to start feeling the wind in her sails—to learn to seek out and use available resources in order to solve her own problems.

0 yes answers

Wow! Impressive. You're one of the few parents possessing the skills and self-control to enable your child to mature and thrive. You have found the ideal balance. Your family understands the value of setting effective boundaries and clear communication. You allow natural consequences to provide opportunity for growth. But that doesn't mean you're totally detached from your child's life—you're supportive and loving while honoring his need for separation. It is not easy to keep yourself from being a helicopter parent. You should be applauded for your "big picture" thinking.

Starting the Rotors in High School

While helicopter parenting might be a relatively new phenomenon for the Millennial generation, "overparenting" has been around for a while. I witnessed signs of it twenty years ago when my hubby and I were first married and experiencing life BK (before kids). We curiously watched our neighbors raise three rambunctious teenage boys. They would share with us the ups and downs of their testosterone-filled home and fascinate us with their creative twists on traditional parenting techniques.

In the spring of their middle son's senior year, word spread around the high school that a group of seniors were hatching a plan to trash the cafeteria during lunch hour. This food fight plan was leaked to administrators, who set clear boundaries and serious consequences: anybody caught participating would be banned from extracurricular activities for the remainder of the year and would not be permitted to walk through graduation ceremonies.

Nonetheless, Operation Food Fight commenced as predicted, and several kids were caught in the act. Fortunately, our neighbor boy wisely chose not to participate—perhaps because he knew his folks were serious about consequences. However, some of his friends did. One boy in particular, a varsity baseball player, was busted practicing his pitching skills with his mashed potatoes.

As warned, he was banned from the remainder of his games and forbidden to walk at commencement. So what did he do? He, of course, called his daddy, who was hovering nearby. Daddy was a local attorney, and he threatened a lawsuit if his boy didn't get to finish out the baseball season and wear his cap and gown.

So what did that student learn? Actions have no consequences. Call Daddy, and he will swoop in and fix it. And the boy certainly didn't learn to respect authority. Do you think this boy—now a grown man—ever developed the skill set to solve his own problems sans Daddy? Did he call Daddy when he received a bad grade in college? Did Daddy always bail him out or threaten the professor? I wonder if he followed his dad's footsteps and became a helicopter parent himself.

In real life, actions do have consequences. And consequences are a vital part of development. So when your child decides to push the boundaries of authority, please remember it is okay—in most cases—to have authority push back. It may go completely against your instincts as a parent, as you want to protect your offspring from discomfort and sadness. But it is often exactly what your child requires to prepare for challenges later in life—or later next year.

Choppers, Snowplows, and Bulldozers

At a university level, helicopter parenting has flown to new heights. In fact, while some parents are helicopters, simply waiting to swoop in and fix any problems, others are snowplows or bulldozers, pushing all obstacles out of the way.

A snowplow parent's mission is to make life as easy as possible for the child by taking care of all needs whatsoever. If the student has to write a paper and study for an exam at the same time, the snowplow parent will "help" by pushing some of the workload away. The parent will do the research for the paper or maybe even write the whole thing. A bulldozer parent is the muscular older sibling of a helicopter parent. A bulldozer parent gets in there and obliterates all obstacles in the child's path. Whether helicopter, snowplow, or bulldozer, these styles of parenting may seem like a good idea at the time but can be quite the opposite for college-aged children.

I had my first real sighting of a collegiate chopper mom when Brooke, then a high school senior, and I took a road trip to Des

Moines so she could audition for a spot in her university's music program. We drove seven hours through a raging Midwest blizzard so she could meet up with a hundred other nervous teenage musicians.

Upon our arrival, I parked myself on a bench along the wall to wait while Brooke stood in line to register and receive her schedule. From my perch, I began to people-watch, curious about these soon-to-be freshmen who could be a part of my daughter's life story.

My eye caught a mother and son entering the building. The mom was toting a large black instrument case in one hand and a thick folder of music in the other. Like the big orange snowplows we'd encountered on our drive, she pushed her way toward the front of the line, announcing her son's arrival to the people at the check-in desk. Her son, empty handed and lagging a few steps behind, didn't say a word. His gaze was focused on the damp, snow-soaked rug the entire time.

I continued to watch as she ushered him to the information table—the one adorned in school colors and loaded with brochures on every aspect of the music program. She instructed him to take some mints from the candy dish. He took two—one white and one blue. She told him to take more. He did. She told him to sit. He did. She read him the itinerary for the day. He listened.

In the short time I observed their interactions, my heart ached for this young man. I knew his mom only wanted to help. But was she actually helping or hurting him? How would this henpecked student ever learn to speak for himself? What would he do in the fall without Mom there to knock all obstacles out of the way? For Pete's sake—how would he know to take more than two mints?

As I observed and waited from the sidelines, we received clear parental instructions for auditions: *no parents allowed.* Only the student auditioning would be allowed in the room with the faculty judges. No exceptions. I took that as my cue to take a self-guided tour of the campus. Giving my anxious daughter a quick good-luck squeeze and a promise to return in two hours, I left. I walked out, knowing this was one step closer to *her* future and *her* independence.

When I returned, Brooke told me every little detail of her audition. There were two professors in the room and one on Skype, as he was stuck in Minneapolis due to the blizzard we'd just plowed through. Brooke admitted she had been nervous the entire time and didn't think she'd done particularly well. When she walked out of her audition room, she noticed a mom (guess which one) in the student-only hallway with her ear pressed onto the door of audition room number six.

Incidentally, Brooke made the band. Apparently she didn't do as poorly as she had thought. And in case you're wondering, the boy with the bulldozer mom made it too. They were in band together that fall. She said he was a talented musician but very awkward. He struggled to communicate. Unfortunately, he dropped out of college after one semester.

Dr. K., a theater professor at a small liberal arts college, shares another example of heavy-handed parenting. The shrill ring of her bedside phone jolted her awake at 11:00 p.m. When she picked up the receiver, she received an earful from an angry parent demanding an explanation of why his daughter hadn't been selected as the lead in the upcoming play. He huffed. He puffed. He threatened action. He promised to pull his future donations from the university.

Dr. K. listened. She explained she'd be happy to discuss the audition process and outcome with his daughter, but not with him. He didn't like her answer. He hung up. And yes, he did contact the university president to threaten action. It's sadly similar to the situation with the boy whose father swooped in after the food fight.

This is a case where lines were clearly crossed. How is the daughter supposed to develop communication skills and confidence when her daddy is fighting her battles? How can she fly when he's stepping on her wings?

Treating College Like a Chevy

Some parents take the helicopter approach merely because they fancy themselves as consumers with the right to demand top-notch customer service. With the price of college tuition rising higher than Kardashian hemlines, many folks now seem to treat selecting and paying for college like selecting and paying for a new car. After kicking a few tires and taking some test drives (i.e., campus visits), your child decides on "the one."

Experts agree that this attitude of consumerism is affecting the college experience. College is viewed as a personal investment and comes with extremely high service expectations. Many parents go into the experience with a "customer is always right" attitude and expect mechanics (i.e., administrators and professors) to be available on a moment's notice. They feel entitled to a menu of extras and personalized attention.

Please don't get me wrong. College *is* expensive. Trust me—I know this firsthand. Our daughter's tuition and room and board is more than double what I made per year at my first job after college. And it's forty times the price of my first car: a Chevrolet Caprice Classic. Paying for college can be a tremendous hardship on family finances. It *is* an investment, of sorts.

But the challenge for parents is to think of college as a group of experiences, not as a product. Understand that no amount of money buys the perfect college experience. If you orchestrate all your child's experiences, where does new learning come from? How will she learn to respond to new, uncharted, unplanned situations? Think back on your own life. When did you learn and grow the most? Was it from the orchestrated experiences? Or was it from the speeding ticket?

University professionals—like most parents—want students to develop the capacities to make wise decisions and navigate the waters of adulthood. They want to help students cultivate healthy relationships. Of course, educators are human (many with children of their own). They understand the parental pull to protect and guide. However, they also worry about how their school climates are affected by intrusive parents trying to set their own agendas.

More so, educators want to help foster, not hinder, students' abilities to develop independence. Educators recognize that a transfer of power is necessary if students are to cultivate the skills necessary to handle the complex demands of modern life. Adolescent dependence on authorities (parents and educators) needs to be replaced with adult responsibility as citizens. Simple, right?

In *Contested Issues in Student Affairs*, researchers Peter Magolda and Marcia Baxter Magolda conclude that in order to achieve significant learning, students must grapple with uncertainty, make mistakes, negotiate, and uphold community standards. Ultimately, when parents and educators step back and leave a student's need unmet, they give the student vital opportunity to learn to meet this need himself.

This plunge into uncharted territory is uncomfortable and downright scary at times—for students as well as their parents. To help parents unfurl the sails, today's universities devote an incredible amount of time and resources to coaching parents to understand the value of autonomy. Freshman orientation sessions incorporate lessons for parents on how to separate from their students, allowing the students to make decisions, appointments, and mistakes so they can grow and learn valuable problem-solving skills. In fact, we'll discuss this next in chapter 3.

The Emperor Moth's Struggle

Parents—even helicopter parents—act from the heart. I too have hovered. Parental involvement is not in itself a problem. I believe most parents—helicopter and otherwise—mean well. Our intentions are pure. We parent with the emotions of love, fear, and hope. Parents are humans. Humans can be both rational and irrational. Humans can love deeply and fear greatly.

So when is parental involvement problematic? When it interferes with the student's development.

Jody Terhaar, dean of students at the College of Saint Benedict, is quick to point out parental involvement is still welcome. "Our aim is not to tell parents to let go completely because, of course, parents are an integral part of their children's lives. We find it effective to discuss how to be involved while still allowing their children to learn the life skills they'll need to succeed in college and beyond."

Terhaar illustrates this with parents on move-in day by sharing the story of the emperor moth. When fully grown, the majestic emperor moth is a sight to behold with its wide wingspan and elegant colors. But before it can become this spectacular insect, it must live as a pupa in a cocoon. The neck of the cocoon is very, very narrow. In order for the pupa to transition into a moth, it must squeeze its way out of the narrow neck.

So the story goes: One day a man found a cocoon of an emperor moth. Curious, he took it home so he could watch it transform from pupa to moth. As he watched, he saw the creature struggle to force its body through the tiny hole. It appeared as if the pupa stopped progressing and was stuck.

Eager to help, the kind man took a pair of scissors and carefully snipped off the remaining bit of cocoon, allowing the moth to emerge easily. The man expected the moth to reveal strong, beautiful wings in which to fly. But instead, it had an awkward, swollen body and small, shriveled wings unable to support its weight. The little moth never did fly. It spent the rest of its short life wobbling around with shriveled wings. After only a few days, it died.

The well-meaning man, in his kindness and haste, actually hurt the creature. He did not understand that the restrictive cocoon is a necessary design. As an emerging moth struggles to pass through the tiny opening, the process forces fluid from the body into the wings to prepare it for flight. In this case, freedom and flight come only after the struggle. By depriving the moth of the struggle, the man had deprived it of health and success.

Just like the moth, our students will, at times, struggle. But the struggles, heartaches, and painful lessons are necessary parts of maturing. Instead of rushing in to fix their problems, let's allow them to struggle and grow. Give them the opportunity to seek advice, problem solve, and develop into healthy, successful adults. Let them grow their wings and fly.

THREE

GETTING YOUR FEET WET

We may have all come on different ships,
but we're in the same boat now.
—MARTIN LUTHER KING JR.

"Welcome to freshman orientation," Bob, a barrel-chested guy with the build of a pro wrestler, said with a chuckle. "Also known as 'bring your checkbook weekend.'"

My husband and I were attending our first parent orientation session on a sunny June afternoon. We and our fellow wide-eyed first-year parents were easy to identify, with our shiny blue binders and crisp Hello My Name Is name tags. While our kids were off navigating the campus with their small groups, we filtered into the campus conference center, past the free coffee and the Welcome Bulldog Parents sign.

Unlike the rest of us, Bob appeared comfortable, even relaxed. We learned he was a veteran college parent, experienced and confident. He was sending his third child off to college. Thus, he had appointed himself the unofficial greeter. Bob knew what to do. If you had a question, Bob had the answer. The rest of us were parental sea sponges, wanting to soak up as much knowledge as we could absorb in ninety minutes or less.

Along with Bob, our welcome committee included a lineup of people representing all aspects of university life: the dean of students, a student health nurse, the director of residence life, the chief security officer, a financial aid guru, a pair of "seasoned" parents, and a few upperclassmen wearing school colors and been-there-done-that smiles. (We'll discuss some of these people later in the chapter.)

As the assistant dean presented the itinerary for the morning, I felt like a first-year student receiving my very first syllabus—overwhelmed yet eager to learn. We were flooded with both information and emotion.

Separate Sessions

Orientation is a time to educate both parents and students on college life. But parents and students often seek different information. (For example, I'm guessing kids are not all that interested in the finer details of the bursar's office.) Universities recognize this and may offer separate orientation sessions for the two groups.

Students will break away into their own groups, often led by specially trained upperclassmen. Their activities include campus tours and casual small-group conversations where current students share personal experiences and give practical advice about everything from favorite professors to hidden gems in the cafeterias. In the summer, your child will likely receive an e-mail regarding orientation as well as placement testing, which at some schools may even be scheduled during orientation. Placement tests give the university an idea of a student's proficiency in particular subjects, such as math and foreign languages.

Parent orientation sessions are usually large-group events with panel discussions and PowerPoint presentations. At our orientation, I took one look at the itinerary and immediately realized this exercise would involve equal parts parental education and letting go. The session would address many practical aspects of student living, such as parking permits, food service options, campus safety, and health services. But it would also address the emotional aspects—the ups and downs of launching our children the first year of college.

Don't Miss the Boat

Why should you attend parent orientation when you're not the one starting college? Why do universities go to such lengths to connect with parents through orientation sessions? Because you play an important role in your student's education.

While it may seem counterintuitive to the "don't hover" messages from chapter 2, your support is valuable to your student's success. During the next few years, you will see your student through an array of emotions and growth. He will struggle with academic responsibilities, experience social conflicts, and question his career choices. Orientation classes can help parents understand and manage expectations for these common college challenges. At orientation, you will learn the best strategies and resources for helping your child through these difficult times.

So don't miss the boat! Plan to attend your orientation sessions. They are a valuable use of your time. You'll pick up helpful nuggets of wisdom and important survival skills for both you and your student.

Staff members are readily available to answer questions about housing, transportation, and degree programs. You'll also get a feel for the culture of the college where your child will spend the next four years. You can familiarize yourself with the lay of the land so you have a general idea of what he's describing when he later mentions "the quad" or "Greek Street." You can reduce some anxiety by knowing where the nearest pharmacy, grocery store, and ATM are located.

What to Expect at Parent Orientation

- **Expect to preregister.** Orientation sessions require a lot of organization on the part of the university. In order to prepare materials, meals, housing (if included), and staffing, they require you to register in advance. Don't be surprised if you're charged a fee to attend. Insider tip: Register early, as certain dates fill faster than others.

- **Expect to ask questions.** Ahead of time, make a list of questions or concerns that are important to you. If they are not answered during your sessions (though they likely will be), you can ask them during a Q&A session or one-on-one meeting.

- **Expect to be overwhelmed.** You will receive a lot of information in a short amount of time. Take in as much as you can, but know it may take some time to process it all. Insider tip: Bring a notebook and pen. Take notes for later.

- **Expect to connect.** You will meet other parents and students embarking on the same journey you are. You will also meet the administrators and staff who will be your student's support system throughout the upcoming years. Insider tip: Take advantage of meet and greets. Your paths may cross again.

Orientation is also a time to connect and cultivate relationships. You'll meet the people who will support your student for the next years of his life. You'll also connect with other parents who share the same excitement and anxieties as you.

Most importantly, you'll connect in a special way to your child. You'll show him you care about this next step in his life and are personally invested in his success.

Different Styles, Same Goal

Most universities have well-planned freshman orientation events. However, each university handles orientation in its own way, with its own style. Sessions vary based on the size and location of the school and when the orientation is scheduled. While their styles may differ, each university's goal is the same: to empower you and your child to have the best possible first-year collegiate experience.

Some universities host orientation sessions during the summer months, often on weekends in June or July, when campuses are less busy. Others take advantage of move-in day or the days prior to the start of the fall semester.

Some colleges use a Welcome Wagon approach. They greet with open arms, showering prospective parents with baskets of goodies in school colors: water bottles, rubber bracelets, bookstore coupons, and a plethora of other useless little logo-adorned plastic bits designed to stir up loyalty and inspire investing in the collegiate community. Others practice what I call the Disney approach. They poise themselves as the happiest place on earth with glossy brochures, roaming mascots, and a souvenir shop where you can purchase previously mentioned logo-adorned bits.

Some schools treat you like cattle, herding you and thousands of others like you—confused yet eager—through a chute into the auditorium for your large-group session. Yet many other universities strive to incorporate the nostalgic vibe of your own collegiate orientation with small, personal breakout groups meeting in lecture halls or classrooms—pep band and cheerleaders optional.

In some cases, freshman orientation will be like a cruise. If this is your first time on a ship, you may be nervous. You may be excited. Your crew, thankfully, will be enthusiastic. The captain, or university president, will welcome you. The first mate will give a safety briefing and show you where the life vests are located. A cruise director will lead you in music (there's no time like the present to learn the school fight song!) or games. You'll probably have food, although it will likely be from a cafeteria. It won't include ice sculptures or champagne, but it usually includes soft-serve ice cream.

You'll learn a great deal and meet other passengers from all walks of life. You'll see the highlights and get just a taste of what's to come for you and your student. You'll leave wanting more.

Getting to Know the Crew

As you cruise through orientation, you'll get a chance to meet many crew members. These are the people supporting your child during her college experience, helping her find success and stay safe during her voyage.

Orientation Counselors (OCs)
Some of the first crew members you and your student will meet are the orientation counselors (aka peer mentors or welcome-weekend ambassadors). The OCs are often the cream of the crop of super-cool upperclassmen at the university. Generally speaking,

they are "experts" on the school, trained to assist your child in his transition. Your child will likely run into these students again. They can be terrific resources for the stuff students really want to know, such as best pizza in town, coolest places to socialize, and an insider's view of residence hall life.

Professors

These teaching professionals are the admirals of the enterprise. The holy grail of your child's academic endeavors. The mojo of the university. They are generally happy to help students enhance their educational experiences—provided the students are actually showing up to class and doing the work. If and when your child struggles in class or has questions about a project, encourage her to make an appointment with her professor or stop in during posted office hours.

Academic Advisors

An academic advisor, usually a professor in your child's chosen field of study, will be assigned to counsel him regarding class selection and offer support throughout the school year. Advisors provide stability as students learn to sail. They help students stay on course with their degree requirements to (hopefully) graduate within four years. (Later in the book, we'll talk about why this is key.) Advisors are experienced educators who understand the system. Your child's advisor can also be an invaluable resource in sorting through internship opportunities and may even be the reference who helps him land an actual paying gig upon graduation.

Resident Assistants (RAs)

RAs are current student leaders who live in the residence halls. Like cruise directors, RAs organize fun dorm activities to encourage students to get to know one another and develop friendships.

While exact job descriptions can vary from school to school, RAs are responsible for fostering a cooperative and considerate dorm environment. RAs monitor dorm life, mediate conflicts, and promote safety. Eastern New Mexico University's RA job description sums it up succinctly, stating the RA's responsibility is "to enhance each resident student's experience by providing information, direction, guidance, friendship, and support."

Student Health Staff

Most universities have a student health clinic on or near campus, providing easy access to services for students. The health staff provides basic health care services, screenings, and education. They focus on the needs of a diverse student population, including disease prevention and lifelong wellness. The student health staff's goal: happy, healthy students making safe, informed choices in and out of the classroom.

Counseling Center Staff

College counselors are experts in the mental health challenges college students encounter, from eating disorders and depression to test anxiety and insomnia. They help students who may be running adrift or concerned about capsizing. The counseling center is a safe, confidential place for students to develop tools to manage stress and improve well-being.

Campus Public Safety Staff

University safety officers work to provide a safe environment on campus 24 hours a day, 365 days a year. They're a visible public safety presence on campus, and they enforce conduct codes and parking regulations. Most campus safety departments believe the best protection against crime is creating an aware and informed community. To accomplish this, they offer educational initiatives and trainings, from self-defense courses to alcohol awareness campaigns. They often provide safety escorts at night and, in some cases, even help jump-start frozen car batteries.

Teaching Assistants (TAs)

These crew members work alongside professors, often assisting or teaching classes. Depending on the university, a TA may teach a class or lab or provide feedback during office hours. For some students, bringing a question to a TA can be less intimidating than approaching a professor.

Dean of Students

The dean of students and related staff members partner with parents and students to help identify and resolve issues keeping students from being successful. Don't let the big title fool you—these folks are approachable and trained to help out in rough waters. They are at the helm of the university and work to resolve barriers that may inhibit student progress. Whether you're concerned about substance abuse or failure to thrive, the staff members in the office of the dean of students are able to offer strategies. If you have a family emergency and need to contact your child or pull him from class, contact this office for assistance and guidance.

During our orientation weekend, we had a special opportunity to meet some of these important crew members. The university hosted a dessert social for the parents and university brass to meet in an informal setting. We mingled over plates of sweets and a glass of wine. (My kind of happy hour!)

Drake's dean of students, Dr. Sentwali Bakari, sat down beside my husband, Marty, and me. He asked if we had any questions or concerns for our daughter as she prepared for her freshman year.

We did. You see, at eighteen, our baby still suffered from

occasional sleepwalking episodes. It gave me my own nightmares of her sleepwalking right out of her dorm building and into the street, with the heavy steel door locking behind her. I'd imagine my little girl waking up outside—alone, disoriented, afraid, embarrassed—and in danger. It was my greatest fear, one that kept me awake at night and made me want to keep her home, where I could protect her.

As we shared this with Dr. Bakari, he waved another man over, the associate university housing director. He too listened to our concerns, then handed me his card and asked if we could follow up in a week, once he had a plan in place. He would, with our daughter's permission, inform the RA and building director of the situation. He would place her in a room near an RA, on an upper floor, and in a centrally located spot away from any exterior doors. Those practical strategies, some of which hadn't even occurred to me in my maternal angst, helped alleviate my anxiety even more than the wine did.

Parent Q&A

Most colleges allow plenty of time for parental questions at orientation events. With our parent session separate from the student session, we had the freedom to ask questions without mortifying our children or receiving their teenaged eye rolls of exasperation.

A friend of mine told me about attending her daughter's freshmen orientation session at a small liberal arts college. Another mom—teetering on the edge of irrationality, like many of us—raised her hand during the Q&A session. She asked how many Catholic churches were in the greater off-campus community. She was concerned about her son not having ample opportunities to worship each week. There was no doubt that continued faith formation was a major priority for this mom—but it was most likely not on her son's radar during orientation weekend.

If you have a Q&A time at your orientation, brace yourself. You will hear every question you never thought to ask—some relevant to your situation, some not. Bring a notebook and jot down notes. From parking permits and tuition payments to on-campus medical services and, yes, faith-based opportunities, you'll be inundated with information. It's a little like drinking from a fire hose!

Be prepared for some interesting questions from interesting folks. For example, I witnessed one mom whip out her list of questions and begin demanding very specific data about degree programs, then followed that with a detailed inquiry about the nutritional content of cafeteria foods. She was leaving no stone unturned!

If another parent's questions seem over-the-top to you, just remember our motto from chapter 1: it's just different. Also remember that no matter how different our parenting styles may be, we are all in the same boat. We are paddling together down the same swirling river of love, anxiety, fear, and hope. When our parental instincts kick in, we're not always rational.

We parents arrive at orientation as a group of strangers from all over the world and from all different backgrounds, representing a wide range of personal and religious beliefs. We leave as a convoy—traveling together in mutual support, united in our collective excitement, anxiety, and love for our children.

After the Q&A, we thoroughly enjoyed getting to know the other parents over burgers and salads in the cafeteria at lunchtime. Conversations ranged from discussing hometowns and move-in day logistics to dating and finances. It was a wonderful mix of practicality and humor.

One dad half-joked to the others, "Just think—our future

sons-in-law could be in this room." Without missing a beat, my quick-witted hubby responded, "Not mine. With what we're paying for Brooke to attend here, I'm hoping hers is already a third-year pharmacy student."

Emotional (Re)Orientation Session

Marty and I, both college educated, had pretty clear expectations of what we'd learn at our daughter's orientation sessions. After all, how much could have changed in a few decades? College is still college, right?

We anticipated lengthy discussion about campus safety and cafeteria plans. We planned to purchase a parking permit and a few college sweatshirts. We expected to learn the schedule for move-in day and the rules of residential life.

But we didn't expect our parenting practices to be challenged. You see, we had barely settled into our folding chairs in the ballroom of the student center when we were told to take a fresh approach to parenting our college students, to reorient ourselves as their mentors. What did this mean?

The panel experts encouraged parents in the audience to "treat your child as if you were a coach or mentor, not a parent." *Not a parent? Hello! We're all parents here!* While the theory had merit, I could sense the estrogen-powered thoughts of the mothers: *Easy for you to say—you didn't push her out after twenty-four hours of labor!*

This emotional reorientation takes a little getting used to, but it makes sense when you look at the big picture of preparing students to handle the problems and challenges of life after college. As discussed in chapter 2, now is the time for a transfer of power and responsibility. We parents need to step back so these young adults can step up.

Jody Terhaar, dean of students at the College of Saint Benedict, explains the college's primary relationship is with *students*, not parents. "We certainly want to partner with parents, but our goal is to empower the student to be her own best advocate. We want to open their minds to new ideas and challenge our students to accept responsibilities for their own choices."

Just how does one "mentor" instead of "parent"? Good question—one that took this mother a while to wrap her brain around. You see, I'm a fixer. I have this innate desire to help people (especially my kids) solve problems. Whether they want my help, I tend to jump in with both feet. To grasp the concept of being a mentor, I looked up the word. Here's what I found:

mentor (noun) an experienced and trusted adviser.

mentor (verb) to advise or train someone (especially a younger colleague).

A mentor is available to listen and advise. A mentor asks thought-provoking questions. A mentor respects the young person's individuality and promotes personal responsibility. A mentor empowers others to learn, grow, and problem solve. Easy, right?

The mentor concept is a challenge for many parents (such as me). Being a mentor means shutting down our rotors. How can we reorient ourselves from well-intentioned helicopter parents to supportive mentors? As we left that orientation session, the control freak in me knew that my daughter was not the only one who would get an education that year. I too had a lot of learning to do!

Experts such as Dean Terhaar realize this mind shift will take time. They offer these suggestions to help parents begin to mentor college-bound kids:

- Make yourself available to listen. Just listen. Don't over-react when she calls about her roommate's boyfriend prancing around their room in his boxers. And remember the anchor theory? Sometimes she needs to simply vent before she can handle the situation herself. Being an anchor in that moment means listening to her spout.

- Ask thought-provoking questions . . . then actually allow your child to answer them. Try saying, "So, honey, how did that make you feel?" and "How are you going to address it?"

- Don't be a fixer. Encourage your student to figure it out and fix it himself. As we discussed in chapter 2, as much as we want to fix their problems, they grow from finding their own solutions.

- Allow your student to learn from her mistakes. Painful? Yes. But very effective. Late papers and missed exams teach valuable lessons.

- Be on a need-to-know status. And that means you *don't* need to know every detail of your child's day-to-day life. Did you talk to your mother every day when you were nineteen? This is yet another part of growth and natural separation.

This emotional (re)orientation session alone was worth our time and effort that June weekend in Des Moines. Parent orientation events are worth your time and effort as well. Attend if you can, even if it isn't mandatory. You'll return home better informed about practical matters and better prepared to parent more effectively. It helps prepare both you and your student for what lies ahead.

FOUR

MONEY MATTERS

I grew to judge every purchase by how many bronze screws I could buy for the boat if I didn't spend on this or made do without that.

—LIN PARDEY

If you're like me, you realize that many things about college have changed since your coed days. If you have a high school senior, your child is probably swimming in a sea of applications, campus tours, and ACTs. His collegiate fan mail may be the cause of your postal carrier's hernia. I'm still flabbergasted at the number of college solicitations our daughters have received. If we had kept them all, we could have wallpapered our entire house with them. Twice.

College is big business. It's not like the old days. Back then, if you had a pulse and a checkbook, you were accepted. Today, college is much more competitive. And expensive. That's true for tuition and room and board, but it's also true about incidentals. University sweatshirts, Chipotle burritos, double caramel macchiato lattes, and so on can add up and surprise us.

This chapter isn't about specific financial aid packages.

Countless other books can guide you and your child down the winding river of financing the college experience of his dreams. For best practices and information on applying for federal student aid, I encourage you to contact the high school guidance office or visit the Department of Education's Free Application for Federal Student Aid (FAFSA) site at fafsa.ed.gov.

Rather, this chapter will focus on how you can prepare your child to make good financial decisions as he embarks on his college voyage. First we'll concentrate on how to teach him about responsible day-to-day money management. His spending decisions today can have potentially huge consequences on his life AC (after college). Our children go to college to grow their minds and prepare for careers, but few (if any) universities teach them how to live in the real world in relation to money. Now's the time to teach him money-managing strategies yourself—before he leaves port.

And after discussing day-to-day money, we'll discuss year-to-year money. That is, we'll take a frank look at the overall effect of student loans, especially when college stretches beyond four years.

Know Your Starting Point

To begin, you'll need a realistic picture of what your child currently understands about money and spending. Does she know how to balance a checkbook? Does she grasp how interest adds up over time? Can she manage a simple budget? Don't just assume your child understands budgets, credit cards, interest, or investments. Unless you've already taught her these things, she likely doesn't know them.

You'll also need a realistic picture of your child's personal perspective on money. Parents and students often have very different expectations on financial management. Considering we have different ideas about almost everything throughout the teenage years, it shouldn't be a shocker! In general, young people often focus on short-term finances, as in, "How can I afford a new dress for the formal next weekend?" Parents, on the other hand, think about long-term, big-picture situations, such as, "How will she ever repay the student loans she's racking up?"

Perhaps your child lives up to these generalizations, or perhaps he doesn't. Now's the time to find out. Has your son worn out the magnetic strip on his debit card from frequent swiping? Or is his hand permanently curled from gripping his first dollar? Does your daughter's pulse race when she sees a Sale sign in the window of Anthropologie? Or has she squirreled away enough babysitting money to pay for a study-abroad semester in Paris?

Understanding your student's financial perspective will be helpful as you move forward. Ask some open-ended questions about finances and review a few of his recent bank statements to get a clearer picture on where your child stands in relation to saving and spending. This will help you determine if you can confirm your child is on a healthy financial track or if you need to address some red-flag behaviors that could lead to future financial trouble.

Little Plastic Cards

Charge! Is that a battle cry or a college student's mantra? It's hard for students to say no to credit cards when they get invitations to sign up with "No Credit History Required!" and "No Annual Fee!" When the company throws in a free gift, all bets are off. Money is tight in college, and some students take the "I'll pay it off when I get a real job" attitude. They don't understand how quickly interest grows.

When Dean and Janet's daughter, Jordan, came home for the

summer following her freshman year, they noticed she received a considerable amount of mail from her friends at Visa and MasterCard. They were mortified to learn that Jordan had opened up six—yes, *s-i-x*—credit cards that year. Jordan herself wasn't concerned. She was making payments on them. Minimum payments only, of course. Dean and Janet immediately scheduled a family finance meeting.

To illustrate the impact those convenient little pieces of plastic could have on Jordan's future, Janet grabbed a piece of paper and a calculator and plotted out the payment plan. Jordan was paying only the monthly minimum—2 percent of the $5,000 outstanding balance, in this case. On a card with a 20 percent interest rate, it would take over fifty-six years to pay off the debt. She'd be almost seventy-five before she would be credit card debt-free. And that was assuming Jordan made no additional purchases in those fifty-six years.

With a few more clicks on the calculator, Janet flashed a number at Jordan: $22,126.13. That was the amount of interest over the fifty-six years. Added together, her $5,000 in purchases would actually cost her a whopping $27,126.13.

The situation opened up a great (albeit late) conversation with Jordan about credit scores, interest rates, payment plans, and future finances. They began by discussing the differences between credit cards and debit cards and how they can be both useful and dangerous to long-term financial independence. If your child doesn't understand one piece of plastic from another, here's a helpful way to describe the differences.

Credit cards (MasterCard, Visa, Discover) are borrowed money. The company issues a card with a specific credit limit—the maximum amount your child can borrow from the company. The biggest advantage of a credit card is flexibility. The cardholder can make purchases without actually having the cash on hand. He has an indefinite amount of time to pay back that money, though a minimum payment is required each month. If managed properly, good credit card use can help build a positive credit score.

The biggest disadvantage of credit cards is the same as the biggest advantage: flexibility. The ease of use and the lack of pressure to pay off the loan makes it very easy to make poor purchasing decisions. When the cardholder doesn't pay off the borrowed amount each month, he is hit with hefty interest charges.

Help your student understand the concepts of principal (amount borrowed) and interest (the rate a lender chargers for a loan) and how interest accrues. The best advice to give your child: pay off your credit card balance in full each month. If you can't afford it at the end of the month, don't charge it. Some people choose to avoid credit at all costs because of the risk of debt.

A debit card, on the other hand, is linked to an existing checking or savings account. When a cardholder swipes a debit card, the money automatically comes out of a checking or savings account to cover the purchase. The money must be in the account in order to cover the purchase. If your student opts for a debit card, you'll want to remind him to keep a close eye on account balances so he doesn't get hit with a costly overdraft penalty.

Debit cards often allow cash withdrawals and deposits as well. By the time they head off to college, many students have already used an automated teller machine (ATM). ATM/debit cards are replacing checks, putting cash at our fingertips.

But these magical sources of cash can create problems for students who don't understand how they work: "Wait—you mean I'm supposed to deduct my ATM withdrawals from my actual checking account?" Again, don't assume your student knows how to balance his debit account if you haven't taught it to him. And if statements come directly to you and not your child, he'll have no way of verifying the balance or knowing if overdraft fees are stacking up.

Speaking of fees, remind your student that transaction fees differ among banks, providers, locations, and accounts. Some banks offer a limited number of free withdrawals per month or have no fees at all. Others charge through the nose for everything. A two-dollar fee for every ten-dollar withdrawal can add up in a hurry!

Encourage your student to contact the institution that issued the ATM or debit card to learn the transaction fee structure. Then have her look for banks on or near campus with low or no fees. Also have her identify the ATMs in her banking network. Lastly, remind your child to use common sense and keep safety top of mind when visiting an ATM, especially at night.

Whether your child uses a credit or debit card is really a personal choice based on personality, maturity, spending habits, and financial needs. There's no right or wrong answer—just what's the best choice for her and your family. Begin by having your student investigate all options available at your local bank, and perhaps do some shopping for a new bank near campus.

Whether she chooses credit or debit, financial tracking is an often overlooked perk to using cards rather than cash. Your student can see exactly how much she's spending and where she's spending it—as long as she reads her online or paper statements regularly.

If your student is responsible and open to the concept of a credit card, many experts believe it is worthwhile for her to apply for one card. Notice I say *one*, not *six*. By using it occasionally and paying off the balances, she can build a positive credit report, allowing flexibility in the future for such things as car loans and mortgages.

We opted to do both a credit card and debit card when our firstborn went off to college. She opened a debit card linked to her personal savings account, and we also opted to add her to our credit card account as an authorized user, mostly in case of emergencies and for agreed-upon incidentals.

If you choose to add your student to your account as an authorized user, be sure to discuss your expectations and restrictions. Don't assume she knows your expectations of what purchases are appropriate. One mom I talked to had discovered to her great shock that her daughter had charged spring break airfare without even discussing it with her parents. Another mom had her card declined at the grocery store because her son had charged enough to flag the account. Don't let this happen to you. Talk to your student and set parameters before it becomes a problem.

You Can Bank On It

Whether your student does her banking at a hometown institution or chooses one near campus is really a matter of personal preference and convenience. If she has a part-time job at school, it may make sense to find a bank near campus for convenience when depositing checks. Or she can look into setting up automatic deposit between her place of employment and her bank.

You can also consider a large national bank with branches in both the student's hometown and near campus. This makes it convenient for parents to deposit into an account at home while allowing the student immediate access to the funds at school. You can avoid snail-mailing checks or long-distance logistics with this process.

University Accounts—Convenience on Campus

Many schools have university accounts where students can

deposit money and use it much like an internal debit card system for campus vendors. In this case, a simple swipe from a student ID badge provides instant access to funds at campus facilities such as laundry, printing centers, food services, convenience stores, and bookstores. As with a debit card, the money must be in the account in order to be spent.

Sounds safe, right? You load the university account, and Junior can buy his books. Just beware that bookstores sell way more than books. Remember the incidentals I mentioned? Bookstores often have a vast selection of clothing, gift items, and, yes, lattes. And for some reason, students may view university accounts as "free money." They don't think twice about swiping their ID cards.

One professor watched a student buy coffees for his entire group of friends, saying, "It's no big deal. My parents are paying for this, anyway." Again, if you're providing financial assistance, please remember to discuss your expectations—unless you don't mind supplying caffeinated beverages for the whole crew.

Cold Hard Cash

When I was a college student home on breaks, Grandma Vesta would give me a hug and slip me a twenty-dollar bill before I left, telling me to have fun. That simple, generous act from a woman on a very tight budget has stayed with me all these years. In those days, a twenty was a lot of money! It not only bought gas but also gave me a night at the movies with both popcorn and soda.

While twenty dollars won't go quite as far today, it is useful for a student to have a small stash of cash for incidentals. How much is enough? That question comes up frequently among parents and is not easy to answer. It depends on the family's financial situation and the student's lifestyle, spending habits, individual needs, and college environment.

Colleen—mom of Jessica, a freshman at the College of Saint Benedict—followed the university's recommendation: she provided Jessica with a limited amount of cash to start the school year, monitored the cash needs over the first few weeks, then adjusted accordingly. They started with fifty dollars cash a month for off-campus meals, movies, incidentals, and gas. Jessica also had access to a credit card for books, haircuts, toiletries, and clothes—as long as she didn't abuse the clothes part. This approach taught Jessica to budget her fifty dollars and recognize that lattes at the Local Blend would have to be a luxury and not a daily event on this voyage. As Benjamin Franklin astutely stated, "Beware of little expenses; a small leak will sink a great ship."

Budgets, Receipts, and Organization

Another part of being an adult and managing finances is proper bookkeeping. I know this isn't sexy stuff. But it's necessary. Consider it another teachable moment, just a little further up the line from how to ride a bike and to not eat glue.

Bookkeeping and budgeting are simple ways to avoid some of the stress tied to money matters. Many student struggle to manage money during college. The broke college student with an inbox full of overdrafts and a cupboard full of ramen is an all-too-common story. According to a 2013 Inceptia National Financial Capability study, 37 percent of students identified finances as a significant source of stress. Also, 31 percent of students admitted to not regularly tracking expenses, and 60 percent had not created a budget for the school year.

See this as an opportunity to help your young adult take better control of her finances and hopefully eliminate some stress.

Teach her how to keep basic records, manage a budget, and set up a simple filing system.

No, I'm not suggesting adding a four-drawer filing cabinet to her already busting-at-the-seams dorm room. I recommend a simple twelve-pocket accordion file, available at any office supply or dollar store. This folder is where your student will file credit card and ATM receipts, bank statements, card statements, university paperwork, tax information, and miscellaneous communication pieces. Many of these items are available online, but even with paperless banking, your student will have some paper to track. This portable file will be easy to haul home if your child has questions or if you need to view a particular file.

Once you purchase the file folder, the very first thing your student should do is photocopy the front and back of each of her credit and debit cards and file them under "Credit Cards." That way, if her wallet is ever stolen, she has the account and phone numbers needed to call and cancel the cards immediately. It is wise for you to keep a second copy in a safe place at home as well.

Good bookkeeping also comes in handy at tax time. Unless you're an accountant, tax paperwork can be confusing for any adult. Don't assume your student understands the process or the paperwork. Yes, another teachable moment. Be sure to explain to your child which records are required for tax purposes. Even if you're paying most of the bills, your student will probably receive some statements and receipts you'll need at tax time.

The key to basic money management is learning to budget. Budgeting provides a realistic picture of spending habits, income, and expenses. It gives students more control of their money while teaching them to be intentional about money use. Plus, getting in the habit of creating and maintaining a budget in college can make it easier to successfully manage more complex finances after graduation.

Another way for today's students to gain financial literacy is to use a money-management application. Yep, there's an app for that. Considering the amount of time he spends with his eyes on a screen, an app may just get him thinking about his financial future. A good budgeting app can help him keep track of finances and help him visualize where he can cut back on spending.

A simple Google search will produce a lengthy list of financial tracking and budgeting applications. One that keeps popping up in conversations with college students across the country is Mint by Intuit. This popular user-friendly app links to a debit or credit card, displaying each transaction both chronologically and categorically. It also allows students to enter transactions for items they buy with cash. While one student called it "the digital equivalent of a nagging mother," he did admit it helped him stick to his budget and made him aware of overspending.

J-O-B: Is it a Four-Letter Word?

College coursework is a student's primary job. However, many students find it helpful (or necessary) to have a part-time job. With the cost of education rising, holding down a job while in school is increasingly common among today's college students.

Some parents are concerned about a job negatively affecting academic success. They don't want their child burdened with job stress on top of school stress, especially if the goal is to graduate in four years.

However, experts say there can be many benefits—aside from income—of holding down a job:

- Broadening connections on campus and in the community

- Developing new skill sets and gaining practical job experience

- Establishing efficient time management techniques

- Expanding a resume and becoming more attractive to future employers

- Building character and work ethic

- Fostering ownership of education by contributing financially

- Making friends

Of course, working during school is beneficial only if the student can properly balance a job and studies. For that reason, it's important to determine the right amount of hours to work each week. That decision really depends on the student's past work experience, time management skills, academic workload, and financial need. Some students may find it best not to take on a job. Others will eagerly take one.

Dr. Laura Perna is a professor at the University of Pennsylvania and author of "Understanding the Working College Student: New Research and Its Implications for Policy and Practice." Her research shows that for students with good time management, working a modest number of hours per week (six to ten hours) won't sabotage a student's academic performance. In fact, some research shows students do slightly better in school when they work. As the saying goes, "busy people get more done."

Avoiding a Lifetime of Loans

We've discussed day-to-day finances. Now let's step back and look at the bigger picture. With the total amount of student debt in the United States reaching a staggering $1.2 trillion, a frank discussion about money would be incomplete without addressing the long-term effects of student loans. While they might not seem like a big deal to your student at the time, loans *are* a big deal. A *really* big deal.

The cost of college is a hot button for most parents. We know college is not getting any less expensive over time. I'll go out on a limb here to assume most parents see their child's education as an investment. They want to feel there's some bang for the buck. Whether your child is attending an affordable community college or a private university where her first semester tuition cost more than your first home, you want her to receive value for the money spent. Also, this is likely true whether your child has worked since fifth grade to fund his own education, whether he's a trust fund baby, or whether you're carefully managing your own assets to help him foot the bill.

Obviously, the level of debt a student or family should take on will vary from family to family. But how much debt is too much for our kids to accrue? Will the end justify the means? These questions tend to crop up in the middle of the night when we can't sleep. We want to help as much as possible, but how?

Of course, the ideal time to discuss the impact of student loans is when students are beginning their college search. By the time you're reading this, you may already be past that point. You may have already weighed the pros and cons of public and private schools and local and faraway schools. You may have already investigated how you'll pay for college expenses in relation to your own personal family financial situation.

But even if your student has already selected a college, you still have another significant opportunity to discuss the impact of loans—and that's right now, when your child is about to embark on her voyage. In reality, the smartest and most effective thing we parents can do to reduce our children's debt burden is to help them recognize the financial benefits of graduating in four years. (Of course, this advice is designed for students in traditional four-year collegiate situations with aspirations of bachelor's degrees. Obviously, some career paths have different instructional requirements.)

Students do not always make the association between the length of time they're in college and the effect it has on their finances. To them, they'll just graduate whenever they graduate. Tuition is often just a number to them, and loans will be paid off "whenever I get a real job."

In reality, there's a lot at stake if your child can manage to graduate in four years. William H. McRaven, chancellor of the University of Texas System, puts this into perspective:

> *To me, the smartest, most effective thing we can do to reduce our students' debt burden is to increase our four-year graduation rates. Common sense tells us that earning a degree in five years is going to cost you roughly 25 percent more than earning it in four. Imagine the uproar if any UT System school increased tuition by 25 percent! But the effect is the same.*

In November 2014, Complete College America published *The Four Year Myth*, outlining these alarming statistics:

- Each additional year of college costs $22,826 for in-state tuition, room and board, and fees.

- Each year also includes $45,327 in lost wages, bringing the total cost to $68,153.

- Only 50 out of 580 public four-year colleges and universities report the majority of full-time students graduate in four years.

Debt increases by nearly 70 percent for students who borrow to attend colleges for two additional years.

This is an area of personal interest for my financial advisor husband. He meets many parents concerned about the financial futures of their recently graduated children. They worry about their children being unable to afford a house or a car. They fear their children will never be able to retire.

My husband knows the consequences of college debt can be dire down the road. Whether a student is choosing between a $25,000- or $60,000-per-year school or considering adding a fifth year, he strongly believes the end result must justify the means (aka the money). Of course, we all want our kids to have the best possible college experience. However, we also need to be realistic.

Crunching the Numbers

We recently had an "end must justify the means" discussion at our house. It was with our younger daughter, who's in the process of selecting a college. Even if your student has already selected a school, you can still gain insight from the principles. It's all about the effect of student loans—specifically, how *additional* costs heap on *additional* debt. You can easily extrapolate the message when guiding your student toward the goal of graduating in four years.

Our daughter has dreams of attending school on the West Coast. She's leaning toward two different universities—with a $9,000-per-year price tag difference between them. To her, the more expensive university offers a broader "experience." (I think that "experience" actually means "closer to the beach.") To help her understand the consequences of the different costs, my husband printed up charts detailing the debt outcomes based on estimated tuition and room and board.

At either university, our daughter will acquire a certain amount of student debt. But if she spent that extra $9,000 a year just for the "experience," the meter would be running at 5.3 percent interest for four years. That would culminate in $39,000 of additional student debt upon graduation. And this in turn would translate into a ten-year repayment schedule of an additional $405 a month—*on top of* her base amount of loans.

How many young people want to start out with an additional $405-per-month bill on top of their existing debt? Is any experience worth paying that much extra? Again, you can also use the same math to determine the additional costs of an additional year of school.

To take it a step further, let's just say our daughter would be lucky enough to land a $40,000-per-year job fresh out of school. Of course, she'd want a place to live, food, a cell phone, Internet, health insurance, car insurance (assuming she already owns a vehicle and is not making payments on one), and gas money. Let's not forget entertainment money, wardrobe expenses, and incidentals. Oh, and taxes.

The reality is, with her baseline amount of student debt *plus* an extra $39,000 in student debt (at $405 a month), even this relatively modest lifestyle would simply not be attainable. On the next page, you can find a sample breakdown of how that extra $405 loan payment might look in a typical monthly budget in the "real world."

The fact is, student loans are often the difference between a young person's financial dependence or independence. I hope this discussion will give you and your child some much-needed perspective before he steps foot on campus. If he hasn't already selected a school, perhaps he'll see the benefit of considering a less expensive college. If he's on his way to school in the fall, perhaps he'll see the benefit of making every effort to graduate in four years. In chapter 10, we'll discuss how to help your student best leverage his college experience (and dollars) to graduate on time for the sake of his future financial well-being.

We know, as parents, that money does matter. It is never more obvious than when we are facing the investment of a lifetime—a college education. Regardless of your individual financial situation, make time to discuss money management with your child. Be real and honest. Whether it's about day-to-day spending, student loans, or part-time jobs, explain how all these factors matter—how they affect life AC and impact long-term financial well-being.

Running the Numbers

Remember our scenario about that additional $405 per month cost? Here's a sample analysis to show your student how extra costs break down. Use this template to introduce the concept of debt load and illustrate the added burden of additional expenses. A realistic financial picture might help the decision-making process.

Feel free to plunk in your own estimated numbers. Expenses, income, and taxes will vary. This chart also does not factor in emergencies (stolen laptop, medical copays), charitable giving, vacations, existing credit card debt, or a nest egg for the future. It also assumes your student already owns a car.

You'll also notice something big missing: the original loan payment amount. In the chapter scenario, the $405 per month was for the extra $9,000 per year the "experience" school cost, compared to the other school. Here, though, let's assume the base expenses have been met between family contributions and scholarships. Of course, not all families can pick up that much of the tab. Again, please fill in your own numbers to get a realistic picture.

Starting Job . . . . $40,000 per year

Monthly Gross $3,333

401(k) Retirement (5%) $167
(although advisors recommend 10% minimum)

Federal Tax (12.5%) $395

State Tax (5%) $158

Social Security (7.65%) $242

NET Take-Home Pay $2,371

Additional Student Loan Payment $405

Rent $800

Utilities $75

Phone $60

Internet $30

Groceries $300

Health Insurance $200

Car Insurance $100

Gas for Car $120

Entertainment $75

Wardrobe $75

Total Expenses **$2,240**

Monthly "Savings" **$131**

PACK THIS ... NOT THAT

At sea, I learned how little a person needs,
not how much.
—ROBIN LEE GRAHAM

Remember in the introduction when I promised practical tips and checklists? Welcome to the practical side of preparing for the freshman voyage. Now is the time to quit humming "Pomp and Circumstance" and start whistling while you work.

This chapter is all about packing for the dorm. (FYI: many universities use the term *residence hall* instead of *dormitory*.) Up ahead, you'll find lists of what to pack and what to leave home. I compiled these lists based on dozens of online collegiate packing lists as well as advice from current students—some who packed well and some who didn't.

But before you head out to Target with your lists in hand, let's take a moment to consider the emotional aspects of packing—for you as well as for your child. After weeks of talking about college, the talking suddenly turns into *doing* as move-in day nears. Packing may seem practical, but it can have a deep effect.

Packing: Therapeutic or Stressful?

The weeks leading up to move-in day are stressful for the entire family. Parents feel the dark cloud of dread—of letting go. Siblings may be eager for their new place in the pecking order, or they may be secretly sad to see their brother or sister move out. And the soon-to-be college student is a ticking time bomb of mixed emotions, ready to explode at the slightest vibration (or shower shoe dilemma—see below).

From a parent perspective, packing for the freshman voyage is a tangible way to send your child off on the right foot. It may be easier to let go if you feel he's prepared and has the items he'll need to function.

I must confess: I actually found list-making and shopping therapeutic the summer BC (before college). I know it sounds crazy, but shopping for twin extra-long sheets helped me feel as though I was doing something productive. It helped me not fixate on the elephant in the room—our daughter leaving. Call it denial. Call it OCD. Call it nesting. Call me Mom. I kept my composure if I focused on the task at hand, such as purchasing pillows and fabric softener, and didn't dwell on the obvious.

Unfortunately, what was calming to me was incredibly stressful for our daughter. As a pile of college stuff began to accumulate in our spare bedroom, bubbling over like a volcano ready to erupt, the reality of this enormous life change engulfed her. One day, I found her plopped in the middle of towering baskets of towels and toiletries—sobbing. She was a mess. Overwhelmed. Crying over shower shoes. Cheap blue plastic flip-flops were her breaking point.

It may be wise to ease into packing gently. Your child (or you) may not be ready for categorized lists and color-coded boxes. As a transition, encourage your student to start with a "college box" early in the summer after graduation. I recommend selecting a plastic tote or a heavy-duty cardboard box. This is where she can start storing things she'll need for college life as she accumulates them or as she thinks about them. For starters, that's where she can place any graduation gifts destined for the dorm—like the lovely embroidered towel set from Great-Aunt Helen.

The college box gives her a chance to start getting organized on a small, manageable scale. It's just one box. It will (hopefully) soon inspire her to get into packing mode—so she doesn't procrastinate and leave all the packing to the last minute.

The Three BEs

Whenever you and your child are emotionally ready to tackle full-scale packing for university life, remember the Three BEs:

BE Organized

When you arrive on campus for move-in day, it will be chaos. (You'll read all about it in chapter 7.) The more you can organize ahead of time, the easier it will be to unpack when you get there. Rooms and hallways are crowded and hot, so anything you can do to make it a smooth move will be in your favor. And while you (and every other college family) will no doubt require a Target run on move-in day, getting organized now will save you trips then, when you'd rather be bonding with your student. Here are some quick organizational tips:

- Prewash all bedding and towels at home before the move.

- Leave hanging items on their hangers, and simply cover them in tall garbage bags. Yes, a garbage-garment bag does the trick. It saves a ton of time, takes up less space, and requires no extra suitcases.

- Pack under-the-bed storage containers with items your student will store in them during the school year.

- Pack like items together. For example, pack toiletries in one tote and food items in another for faster unpacking.

- Label each box and bag with your child's name, building, and room number in case something gets misplaced upon arrival.

BE Realistic

Dorm rooms are more likely to resemble Gilligan's quarters on the *S.S. Minnow* than the ballroom of the *Titanic*. Remember how small the dorm room was when you toured it? Rest assured—it didn't grow. Keep this in mind as you pack, and remind your child of it before you decide to rent a U-Haul to bring her stuff to school.

BE Smart

Read through the residence hall rules prior to packing. There's no need to purchase (and haul) a coffeemaker with exposed heating element or toaster if fire codes or university policies prohibit them. Also, have your student discuss larger items (futon, fridge, TV) with his roommates ahead of time so you don't lug a futon up four flights of stairs only to find out the roommate already has one there. Bonus: It starts a dialogue between the new shipmates—they have a whole year ahead of them of learning how to work things out.

Dorm Decor

Your student may be less than thrilled to pack for the dorm. But packing is one thing; dreaming about the decor is another.

If you're the parent of a college-bound daughter, you've probably spotted multiple copies of PBdorm catalogs from Pottery Barn conspicuously tucked around your house. Don't fret; this is normal behavior. Young women are sucked in by the coordinating sets of "dorm room essentials" and stylish (i.e., expensive) shower caddies. They are enamored by chevron-patterned pillows and matching desk lamps. Our daughter was no exception. However, we quickly pointed out that she had Pottery Barn taste and a Target budget!

Guys are usually less concerned about stylishly themed décor, but that doesn't mean they don't have ideas for their dorm rooms as well. Don't assume he'll just assemble a fashionable pile of dirty clothes to decorate the space—at least not for the first few weeks, when he's trying to make a good impression. For most guys, decorating means two things: practicality and simplicity. Oh, and electronics. Yes, an Xbox 360 does count as a bare essential for your gamer.

If you're like me, you'll want to show your love by outfitting his dorm room. Again, this is one way you can feel useful and necessary as he prepares to move out. When you look at him, you may see the little boy in *Toy Story* pajamas, not the young man about to set out on his own. As emotional as this may be, try to resist the urge to buy him the navy plaid comforter set, complete with matching throw pillows and dust ruffle, without at least consulting him first.

Whether your student is a budding interior designer trying to achieve a contemporary-modern vibe or whether she is simply shooting for a lived-in look, give your college-bound kid the freedom to personalize the space—within a reasonable budget. This task teaches the delicate balance of blending personality, individuality, and practicality.

Moving into the dorm room is one of your child's first fleeting steps into this new collegiate life. No matter how it is decorated, keep in mind that your child will call it home for the next nine months.

The Lists: Pack This . . . Not That!

Get out your highlighters and pens, folks. Here are the lists for what to pack and what to leave at home. While I've done my best to provide thorough lists, they're by no means complete. Not every item is necessary for every student. Consider them a starting point. You and your child can and add (or delete) items as you go.

And if you're the type wide awake all night with lists swirling around your head, just remember: unless your child is heading to college in Siberia, there's probably a CVS or Target just around the corner for forgotten odds and ends. Anything else can be ordered later online and delivered to the residence hall.

Pack This!

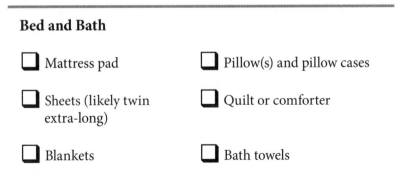

Bed and Bath

- ☐ Mattress pad
- ☐ Sheets (likely twin extra-long)
- ☐ Blankets

- ☐ Pillow(s) and pillow cases
- ☐ Quilt or comforter
- ☐ Bath towels

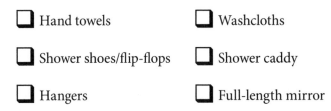

☐ Hand towels   ☐ Washcloths

☐ Shower shoes/flip-flops   ☐ Shower caddy

☐ Hangers   ☐ Full-length mirror

Please confirm the size of your student's bed, as most universities use twin extra-long mattresses. No amount of stretching or pulling will make regular-sized sheets fit. Also, the room will not have a linen closet. Many students suggest packing only one set of sheets. "I just take them off to wash them and then put them right back on the bed," explains Alex, a freshman. "Why use up space storing a spare set?" she adds. Another general consensus from students: Communal showers are gross. Bring shower shoes.

Laundry

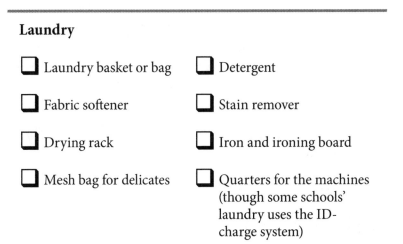

☐ Laundry basket or bag   ☐ Detergent

☐ Fabric softener   ☐ Stain remover

☐ Drying rack   ☐ Iron and ironing board

☐ Mesh bag for delicates   ☐ Quarters for the machines (though some schools' laundry uses the ID-charge system)

Check your student's resident hall information page regarding laundry facility specifics. Many times, students can check out irons and ironing boards from the front desk.

Cleaning Supplies

☐ Antibacterial wipes   ☐ Glass cleaner for mirrors

☐ Dish soap   ☐ Paper towels

Again, check your student's resident hall information page. Many residence halls let students check out vacuum cleaners, brooms, and other cleaning supplies.

Personal Hygiene Supplies

☐ Shampoo and conditioner   ☐ Brush and comb

☐ Styling products   ☐ Styling tools (hair dryer, flat iron)

☐ Toothbrush and toothpaste   ☐ Mouthwash

☐ Razor and shaving accessories   ☐ Makeup

☐ Sunscreen   ☐ Moisturizer

☐ Nail clipper and file   ☐ Nail polish and remover

☐ Cotton balls and Q-tips   ☐ Tissues

☐ Soap and container for soap   ☐ Feminine supplies

First-Aid Kit / Medicine Chest

☐ Prescription medications

☐ Antacid

☐ Cough relief (drops, syrup)

☐ Cortisone cream

☐ Bug spray

☐ Antiseptic wipes

☐ Thermometer

☐ Copy of health insurance card

☐ Pain relief (acetaminophen, ibuprofen)

☐ Allergy meds

☐ Antibiotic ointment

☐ Band-Aids

☐ Condoms

☐ Ice pack

☐ Tweezer

☐ Storage container for medical items

These items are merely suggested products and certainly not meant to replace a visit to a health care professional. Also, a pharmacist friend of mine recommends including a sheet of instructions about what to use for a particular ailment and how to do so safely. Her advice: you've likely handled the distribution and dosage of your student's medications for the past eighteen years, so please don't assume she automatically knows what to do with them now. Don't send your child off to college with all of the meds and none of the wisdom!

Electronics

☐ Power strip with surge protector (UL approved)

☐ Alarm clock

☐ Laptop and charging cord

☐ External hard drive or other data storage

☐ Flash drives

☐ Ethernet cable

☐ Cell phone and charging cord

☐ Camera

☐ Music player

☐ TV (plus remote and user manual)

☐ TV coaxial cable

☐ Blu-Ray/DVD player (plus remote and user manual)

☐ Gaming system

☐ Printer, ink, and paper

Customize this list of electronics as needed. With smartphones being all-in-one devices, your student may be able to delete several items from the list.

School Supplies

☐ Sturdy backpack

☐ Desk lamp and lightbulb(s)

☐ Pens and pencils

☐ Notebooks

☐ Calculator

☐ Scissors

PACK THIS . . . NOT THAT

☐ Stapler   ☐ Scotch tape

☐ Post-its   ☐ Calendar

☐ Adhesive products safe for walls

To avoid damaging the walls and getting fined at the end of the year, invest in adhesive products safe for painted surfaces. I highly recommend 3M Command strips and 3M ScotchBlue painter's tape. I promise I'm not a spokesperson for 3M. I just happen to know these products really work. The Command line includes hooks of all sizes. They are great for holding everything from pictures and hats to robes and towels. They also make strips that work for hanging posters or heavier mirrors. They're not cheap, but in my opinion, they're worth every penny.

Food Stuff

☐ Microwave   ☐ Mini refrigerator

☐ Plastic food storage containers with lids   ☐ Plastic food storage bags

☐ Microwave-safe plates and bowls   ☐ Silverware

☐ Plastic cups and glasses   ☐ Can opener

☐ Refillable water bottle(s)   ☐ Insulated coffee mug with lid

Most students have meal plans through the residence hall and may never make more than microwavable popcorn on their own. In other cases, though, residence halls have shared furnished kitchens, where your student can channel her inner Julia Child. Others have smaller unfurnished kitchenettes, where students must supply their own cookware. Be sure to find out what your student's hall has to offer.

Also, review the university's housing policies before investing in a refrigerator, as some have strict requirements on size. It's no fun to haul a too-large fridge across the state and up several flights of stairs only to return home with it in your trunk. Some colleges rent out appliances such as mini refrigerators and microwaves. It may be wise to check online and compare costs between buying and renting.

Miscellaneous

☐ Assorted storage totes and tubs

☐ Fan

☐ Rug

☐ Umbrella

☐ Reference books (*Elements of Style*, *MLA Handbook*, etc)

☐ Sports equipment (Rollerblades, bike with sturdy lock, helmet, rackets, balls)

☐ Photos

☐ Posters and room decor

Identification / Medical / Financial

☐ Driver's license

☐ Auto insurance card

☐ Prescription card

☐ Health insurance/HSA card

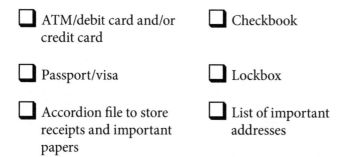

- [ ] ATM/debit card and/or credit card
- [ ] Checkbook
- [ ] Passport/visa
- [ ] Lockbox
- [ ] Accordion file to store receipts and important papers
- [ ] List of important addresses

Theft does happen on a college campus, but keep in mind most dorm thefts are crimes of opportunity. (See chapter 13 for more discussion.) Some universities provide a small locking cabinet or drawer as part of the dorm room furnishings. One question that crops up frequently on parent portals and college websites is whether to invest in a personal safe or lockbox for the dorm—a place to lock up cash, passports, personal information, and prescription drugs. Some parents respond with a resounding "Yes!" They find value in the added security, especially for the student's prescription meds. Other parents deem the investment unnecessary. "I totally believe the safe is for the parents' peace of mind and is not necessarily something the student wants or will use," says Gwen, a mom of two college-aged boys. With mixed reviews like these, you'll have to do your homework and make the decision that you feel is best for your student.

Clothing

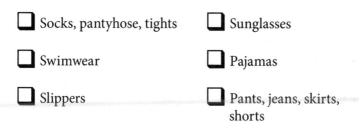

- [ ] Socks, pantyhose, tights
- [ ] Sunglasses
- [ ] Swimwear
- [ ] Pajamas
- [ ] Slippers
- [ ] Pants, jeans, skirts, shorts

☐ Shirts, sweaters, jackets ☐ Fitness wear

☐ Formal/business attire ☐ Rain gear

☐ Cold-weather gear (winter boots, coats, hats, and gloves)

Depending on your child's affinity for fashion, clothing can challenge your packing prowess. Students tend to overpack. If he's running out of wardrobe space, divide his clothes by seasons. For example, have him pack his summer and fall clothes for move-in day, then have him pack a box of winter clothing to set aside at home for later. If you plan to visit him at some point, you can bring him the next season's box, or he can plan to swap out seasonal boxes if he'll be home during breaks.

Not That!

☐ Social security card (have your student memorize the number)

☐ Candles or incense

☐ Amplifiers

☐ Electric blankets

☐ Extension cords

☐ Halogen lamps

☐ Hot plates/hot pots

☐ Coffee maker with exposed heating element

☐ Toaster (depends on the university fire code)

☐ Space heaters

☐ Weapons

☐ Rope/string lights (depends on the university fire code)

☐ Latex balloons (due to allergies, many halls are latex-free)

☐ Pets (even monkeys— see chapter 7)

Before purchasing certain items, take a close look at your child's housing packet to learn about the university's fire codes. I was surprised to see hot pots, coffee makers with exposed elements, and toasters on the "do not pack" list when our daughter received her initial housing packet. As a coed of the '80s, I have fond memories of burning Kraft Mac & Cheese to a crisp in my orange hot pot. But fire codes in several states now prohibit the use of anything with an exposed heating element in residence halls. Fire codes may also restrict string lights and extension cords.

If your caffeine-powered offspring already appears to be catapulting into a full-blown panic about not bringing his favorite coffee maker, let him know that many places do allow Keurig-type coffee makers, which do not have an exposed heating element. And if that isn't enough reassurance, please explain that caffeinated beverages are readily available on or near every college campus.

CAMPUS NAVIGATION

*The wind and the waves are always on the side
of the ablest navigator.*
—EDMUND GIBBON

As move-in day approaches, you'll find yourself in full-blown packing mode, checking items off your list with confidence and precision. Just make sure you don't overlook a very important packing decision: Do you send your child off to school with a car, a bike, or a pair of Nikes? That is, how will your child get from class to class? How will he get to a grocery store or come home on weekends?

Now's the time to sit down with your student and discuss transportation around and beyond campus. Once you weigh all the options, you'll have a clearer sense of whether he should make the trek with his car or leave it back home.

Boots, Blades, and Bikes

You might want to remind your child that his everyday transportation needs will be relatively simple. Most days, he'll go from the dorm to classes to the library to the coffee shop and back to the dorm.

Many students simply hoof it around campus with the help of Nike, Adidas, or Puma. Depending on the campus's size and amenities, your child may be in walking distance from not only classes but also all his shopping, dining, and entertainment needs. A pair of good sneakers (or warm boots, depending on the university's location) is all that's required. At a larger school, Rollerblades are a speedy option when the weather cooperates.

Walking is not only free but healthy. It can even help prevent the freshman fifteen. Some students get a kick out of tracking their daily steps on a Fitbit or other pedometer-type tracking device or app. A little motivation can't hurt, right?

As always, safety must come first when walking or blading. Remind your student to pay attention to her surroundings and to never walk alone at night. You may get the eye roll as you state the obvious, but these instructions bear repeating to a teen who thinks she's invincible. See chapter 13 for more student safety tips.

Biking is also a popular option for students. Many cities and universities promote and readily support bicycling on campus by offering bike-sharing programs. For example, the University of Minnesota, in partnership with the City of Minneapolis, launched a public bike-sharing system back in the fall of 2010, and it is still providing opportunities to pedal today. The purchase of a season pass allows students to check out bright-green bicycles from public kiosks and return them to multiple locations on and near campus. With a large campus covering 1,204 acres, bikes are a big deal at the U of M. The quad areas between buildings on this bike-friendly campus have clearly marked bike lanes painted on the concrete, like a mini interstate for cyclists.

But before you go and strap the ten-speed to a makeshift bike rack on the family sedan for move-in day, your child should first check out his university's bicycle policies. Some universities offer special bike storage options and even classes on building cycling confidence, staying safe, and navigating campus. Also, it is wise to invest in a sturdy lock, as bikes are prone to theft on many campuses.

If a bicycle is your child's preferred method of transportation, make sure he realizes it has limitations. For instance, it can be challenging to balance a bag of groceries, a backpack, and a six-pack on a bike. It can also be challenging to ride a bike through slush and snow. For the times when a bike isn't an option, your child will need to go on foot or catch another ride.

Bike Theft Prevention

Here are some tips to pass along to your student if she's bringing her bike to school.

- Bring an inexpensive bike to campus.

- For maximum protection, use a U-lock.

- If you have quick-release hubs, don't forget to lock your wheels and seat post.

- Always lock your bike, even if you'll be gone for just a minute.

- Park in a well-lit area.

- Write down your bike's serial number for matching in case of theft.

- Alert the police of any suspicious activity.

Campus Shuttles

Is your child attending a geographically large university? Many large campuses provide free on-campus shuttle systems for students.

Depending on the university, shuttles can run from very early in the morning (for those overzealous freshmen who signed up for an 8:00 bio lab) to late at night (to accommodate the nighttime library study hours). Generally safe and reliable, these shuttles are designed with students' needs in mind.

The University of North Dakota, for example, has a shuttle that runs across campus from approximately 7:30 a.m. to 10:30 p.m. on weekdays. To accommodate the large number of aviation students who need access to the training facility at the Grand Forks airport, UND also provides an airport shuttle seven days a week. There's also an app that provides real-time updates about arrival times, schedule changes, service disruptions, or traffic delays. During frigid North Dakota winters, students certainly appreciate knowing if a shuttle is running late. It saves them from standing outside while their eyelashes freeze together. (Yes, it actually happens. Eyelashes do freeze. Just ask any student who has survived a North Dakota winter.)

Public Transportation

Remember the song back when your freshman was your toddler? *The wheels on the bus go round and round . . .* This may be the time to reintroduce that bus—or the subway or train system. Public transportation is definitely worth exploring if your student is in an urban area without a car and wants access to shopping, groceries, and off-campus jobs.

Many cities offer user-friendly public transit options with discounted rates for students. A simple Internet search will provide available routes and schedules. Look into student discounts or monthly passes if your child will be using the system frequently.

Of course, depending on the city, you'll also want to do a little research about the quality of the transit system. As one student explains, "While riding the city bus sounds good in theory, it is not always as safe, efficient, or dependable as the brochures make it sound." If possible, have your child talk with students who have used the city's public transportation. When you're in town for orientation, take a test ride with your student, if you have the time and inclination. Buy a couple of bus or train passes and check it out together. This will give both you and your child firsthand knowledge of the process, convenience, and safety of public transportation in the community.

In addition to public transportation, taxi cabs are available in metro areas. Taxis can be good options for some occasions—such as heading to the airport or going with the gang to an all-ages nightclub—but they can be somewhat pricey for students. Other options such as Lyft or Uber make cities more accessible for students, often at a reduced cost. These on-demand car services are gaining popularity. They allow students to request private drivers through apps on iPhone and Android devices. Of course, as with any transportation service, basic safety protocols and common sense must be practiced when securing rides in unfamiliar areas.

Bringing Your Own Wheels

Considering all the transportation options your child has around campus, should you send her to college with a car? That's a question only you can answer. Some families find it unnecessary.

Others find it convenient, especially if the student plans to make trips across town and come home often.

Many factors play into whether to send her with wheels. However, some colleges make the decision for you: they do not allow freshmen to have cars on campus. This topic is often addressed at orientation sessions, where you will learn about university vehicle policies, parking lot locations, fees, and restrictions.

If little Jenny has inherited the family Chevrolet and is thinking about having it with her on campus, you have many things to consider.

- How often will she actually use the car? Does she need it for working off campus?

- Does she need a car to come home? How often? If she doesn't have a car, how else will she get home?

- Will she be in a large urban area where parking is outrageously expensive and not readily available? Or does the university have safe, affordable lots near the residence halls? Is the parking lot secure, or is it especially vulnerable to theft or safety issues?

- Is gas and upkeep affordable? Is she able to handle basic maintenance and care of a vehicle?

- Is the car reliable and safe? Or is there a chance it will leave her stranded on the side of some road?

- If the university is located in a winter wonderland, is she willing to get on the business end of a shovel and dig out the car during the snowy months? Is she willing to follow parking policies for removing cars prior to snowplowing?

Before You Hand Over the Keys

If you decide to send your child off with a car, you have many issues to address prior to move-in day. There are rules, protocols, information, and options to discuss up front. As always, don't leave anything to assumption.

- **$$$:** Cars require gas. Gas costs money. A lot of money. Decide now who fills the tank.

- **Protection:** Is AAA a smart investment for your family? OnStar? GPS unit or app? These are all options to consider if your child is moving far from home or driving in a frigid climate.

- **Insurance coverage:** This is a wise time to review your policy with both your agent and your child.

- **Driver's seat:** Who can drive the car? Only your child? Roommates? Friends? Don't assume he knows your wishes. Discuss how he will answer requests to borrow the car.

- **Busted:** Clearly identify who pays for speeding citations, parking tickets, and towing fees *before* the situation arises. Trust me—it will.

- **Deal breaker:** *Do not drink and drive.* This rule needs to be stated clearly. Tell your child it is nonnegotiable.

Goober's Basic Self-Service

Does your child know some basic car care? I'm not talking oil changes or belt replacements here. Just the basics. If your child doesn't already know how to handle these simple maintenance tasks, head out to the garage for some automotive 101.

- How to fill the gas tank

- How to check the oil level, and how often (and where) to get an oil change

- How to monitor tire pressure and fill with air, if necessary

- How to safely change a tire—or at least whom to call—in the event of a flat

- How to safely jump-start a car

- How to open a frozen car door

- How to add antifreeze (Can you tell we live in the upper Midwest?)

Friends with Wheels

Unless it's a school with a no-car policy, your child will likely know someone with a set of wheels, even if he leaves his own wheels at home. If so, he may be lucky enough to carpool and bum rides with pals. Carpooling may be a convenient option when your student needs to head across town for shopping or a special event. Just make sure to teach your child proper etiquette about chipping in for gas and other considerations.

Carpooling, whether with friends or through the university services, is also a convenient option when your student heads home. Gone are the days of hitchhiking home for the holidays. During breaks, some universities provide shuttles to local airports. Other colleges coordinate (for a fee, of course) motor coach transportation to regional drop-off points, so parents can pick up their students closer to home.

Gone too are the days of a bulletin board in the dorm hallway with "Need a ride to Saint Cloud on April 3. Will pay for gas." Today, that bulletin board has gone high tech. While some students still rely on old-fashioned word of mouth to garner rides, many use Facebook and Twitter. Some universities offer online boards to connect drivers with riders.

Sally, a student at Saint Scholastica in Duluth, Minnesota, used her university's freshman Facebook page to connect with other students driving to her hometown of Saint Cloud. "My mom kept telling me to put a note on a bulletin board, and I tried to explain to her that's not how it's done anymore," she said. Through classes and dorm activities, Sally met several other students from the Saint Cloud area. Now she has more available rides than weekends. "Anybody who is driving that far alone is happy for company and some gas money," she explains.

Gas money and companionship. That's what friends are for.

PART

TWO

ANCHORS AWEiGH

SEVEN

BON VOYAGE

A ship in harbor is safe,
but that is not what ships are built for.
—J. A. SHEDD

As our two-car caravan made its way down I-35 on move-in day, I felt a nostalgic pull back to the summer after her third grade year. At nine years old, she was already eager to experience new things. A week at summer camp three hundred miles away was just the ticket.

The parallel was not lost on me. On move-in day, our car (and my mind) was filled with the same intense combination of excitement and anxiety and independence as it had been nearly a decade earlier. And those emotions became even more intense as road signs indicated our arrival at the Iowa border. Her new state. Her new address. Three hundred miles from home.

We arrived on campus along with what seemed to be a million other overloaded vehicles. The streets and parking lots were full, and the sidewalks were bustling with dazed parents and distracted students.

As we pulled up to the curb in front of Carpenter Hall,

energetic people in brightly colored matching T-shirts greeted us—just like at camp. They were all smiles, clipboards, enthusiasm, and muscles. Before we had time to grasp the moment, these upper-classmen tagged and unloaded Brooke's belongings into a mound on the sidewalk and asked us to move our car. We returned to find the mound shrinking, with another team of sweaty students schlepping her stuff up to her third-floor room. This move-in crew was amazing—a one-time perk for first-year students and parents.

Grabbing the last few totes and boxes, we made our way up the stairs along with approximately a thousand other people. I had to chuckle at the number of sweaty dads wearing Drake T-shirts, embracing college culture and showing their support. Clearly, it was a lucrative day for the university bookstore's cloth-ing department!

We rounded the corner and stopped in our tracks, blocked by a mountain of futons, fridges, boxes, bags, totes, and bedding in the hallway. There was no way around it, and I was too old to climb it. Fortunately, Brooke's room was the closest to the stairwell. Then we realized it was *her* mountain of futons, fridges, boxes, bags, totes, and bedding we needed to dismantle.

And we did, one tote at a time. We had arrived before her roommate, which actually made moving in a bit easier. It allowed a little more space to unpack. Later, we were able to get out of the way when her roommate arrived with her parents and her own mountain of stuff.

My maternal instincts surged as we began to unpack boxes. I wanted to show my love by making her bed and organizing her drawers. However, these were things she wanted—no, she *needed*—to do herself. This was her moment, not mine.

While fighting the urge to fold her socks, I had a flashback to the separation anxiety she experienced as a toddler. Any time I had to leave her, Brooke would cling to my leg and look up at me, her lip quivering and her big blue eyes pooling with tears. Now that separation anxiety was all mine. (We'll talk about this even more in the "Changing Course at Home" chapter coming up next.)

Move-in day—you've been working toward this moment all summer (or longer). This chapter, like many chapters, covers both the emotional and the practical aspects. Later, we'll talk about how to be smart and efficient as you unpack. But first, let's get to the heart of the matter.

Emotional Spectrum

By now, you have a pretty good idea of my mental state as we moved in our daughter. I was a volatile blend of fear and excitement. Not all parents feel this way.

One mom revealed she was secretly glad to see her daughter head off to college, as she'd been such a pill to live with all summer. Another mom was totally chill about move-in; however, her daughter was attending school ten minutes from home. A dad who was dropping off his third child had the process down to a science with very little concern.

We each handle this transition differently. Just as no two college students are the same, neither are their parents. There's an emotional spectrum on move-in day. You'll see plenty of parents with red eyes and Kleenexes strategically shoved up their sleeves. You'll also see folks in "business mode," checking off tasks from their to-do lists, saving their tears for the car ride home.

You may find yourself like me, wanting to funnel your emotions into action as you unpack. As challenging as this may be for parents (moms in particular), please allow your student to set the tone and pace of unpacking. There is ownership and validation in his own nesting. I'm not suggesting you need to leave him and his mountain in the hallway. But you don't need to take charge. Instead, just ask what you can do to help.

You'll likely get assigned the tasks of lofting beds and hanging mirrors. You may even get to haul boxes out to the recycling dumpster, if you can scale the other mountains in the hallway. If you do make it out to the dumpster, you'll likely meet up with other displaced parents fighting the same feelings of helplessness. Take time to say hello. You'll likely find an ally.

But also be prepared to see all types of parents on move-in day. Some are, shall we say, in a category of their own.

As we were schlepping our daughter's things up the three flights of stairs, we encountered many other parents-turned-pack-mules in the stairwell. On one trip, I did a double-take as a fashionably dressed mom and son passed by. The mom was wearing an interesting furry scarf around her neck. *Odd*, I thought. After all, it was August in Iowa, and the residence hall did not have air conditioning. Fragrant hallways and pit stains were the norm, so a fur scarf was most unexpected.

Then it moved. The scarf moved. I wasn't having a hot flash or a hallucination. It actually moved.

I turned to my daughter to make sure I hadn't imagined it. "Did you see that?" I asked.

I looked again. The woman had a real, live monkey on her neck as she trudged the stairs of Carpenter Hall. I'm not kidding.

Confused, Brooke simply replied, "I didn't know monkeys were allowed in the dorms."

We didn't know if the monkey was simply along for the fun on move-in day or if the student intended on keeping it in the dorm as some sort of floor mascot. If the latter, then the RA nixed the idea, because Brooke didn't see the scarf monkey in the hall again that year. If the former . . . well, while it made for an interesting sight on move-in day, I recommend parents leave pets at home. Even monkeys.

Monkey or no monkey, remember that we all approach move-in day in our own way. No matter what kind of parent you are, cut yourself some slack. Move-in day is a big deal.

I do want to offer you a glimmer of hope: as a parent who survived her child's freshman year, I promise you the second-year drop off will be far less dramatic.

A Tangible Good-bye

When it comes time for you to leave, try your best to not project your angst. Your child will have enough of her own. Instead, remind her how proud you are of her. Compliment her independent spirit. Show your support with positive, uplifting words. Those words of confidence create a ripple effect that will remain once you've gone home.

That is, if you can get those words out. I knew I'd be a mess when it came time to leave. After all, I'd been both dreading and anticipating this day since I helped her pick out her first-day-of-school outfit for kindergarten. How could I possibly put my feelings into words? Would I even be able to muster up the words when the time came? Doubtful. So, the morning of "The Day," I sat down and wrote my baby girl a note. I poured my heart out onto a page of white paper. You can find the letter at the end of the book.

I highly recommend doing this if you're prone to clamming up when you're emotional or if you know you'll be a blubbering mess unable to grunt out the words you're thinking. Write a note of support ahead of time, and leave it on your child's pillow.

Even if you feel confident in being able to express your message in a meaningful way, there's still a benefit to writing a letter. Your child can read and reread the letter whenever he needs to feel your loving support. It'll be an instant "hug" from home.

And once you've said your good-byes, *go home*. Leaving is inevitable. Prolonging it helps nobody. Your child may cry—or may not. Either way, he needs to go meet his new neighbors and begin his new life as a college student. The university will engage the students almost immediately, keeping them too busy to dwell on sadness.

Smooth Sailing on Move-In Day

That's the emotional end of things. Now let's get down to the brass tacks—or more appropriately, the 3M Command strips. Here are some practical tips for smooth sailing on move-in day.

- **Book a room in advance.** If you're arriving from a distance and plan to spend the night before move-in day in a hotel, make your reservations early. Very early. Rooms tend to fill up quickly on move-in weekend. (Bonus tip: Same goes for family weekend and homecoming.)

- **Load the night before.** Please, please, *please* don't pack up the minivan the morning of move-in day. The day is exhausting enough without the added stress of playing packing Tetris at 5:00 a.m. before you hit the road. Plus, if her stuff doesn't fit into the vehicle, it probably won't fit into her dorm room. Doing it the night before gives you time to edit if necessary.

- **Do your homework.** Read the move-in day materials from the university. Does her building have elevators or stairs? Were you assigned a specific move-in time slot? Where should you park to unload the vehicle? Where does she check in and get her key and ID card?

- **Bring your paperwork.** Place all relevant paperwork (student ID number, check-in times and locations, campus map, parking information) in one easy-to-access file.

- **Bring a tool kit.** It's helpful to have a simple tool kit (hammer, screwdrivers, pliers, scissors, etc.) as well as a rubber mallet to assist in lofting beds and assembling furniture. Plus, it gives you something to do with your hands while your student unpacks. And let's face it: there's nothing like assembling IKEA storage cubes to occupy your mind (or challenge your sanity).

- **Wear comfortable shoes and clothing.** And deodorant! Move-in day is not a fashion show and definitely not the day to break in a new pair of shoes or wear your new white pants. Keep in mind that in many parts of the country (even the upper Midwest), temps often soar at that time of year. As you haul boxes and fridges, plan to break a sweat. And plan to get dirty. Dorm rooms may require a wipe down before the unpacking begins. (There's a good chance this might be the only time that room is actually cleaned the entire year!)

- **Expect the unexpected.** Not all schools have a streamlined move-in process. Some take a free-for-all approach, while others have very specific schedules and rules, including time allotments for parking in front of the building. No matter what approach your student's school uses, expect some chaos. Elevators break. Lines of communication can too. Between logistics and emotions, the likelihood of something going awry on move-in day is very high. If you go into it expecting the unexpected, you'll be able to handle whatever comes your way with grace.

- **Bring your Target charge card.** In spite of ever-so-careful planning and checklists, your child *will* forget something. You and hundreds of other college parents will jockey for parking spots at Target and wonder why you never previously purchased stock in Target or 3M (see chapter 5).

- **Remember to eat.** In all the excitement—and chaos—of moving in, folks sometimes skip meals. The combination of unpacking, low blood sugar, and high emotions is a recipe for disaster. Arrive prepared with some cold drinks and snacks.

- **Reap the fruits of your labor.** If you followed the tips in chapter 5, then unpacking should be a relative breeze. This is when you'll reap the benefits of prewashing the bedding and towels, leaving clothes on their hangers, using under-the-bed storage containers, packing like items together, and clearly labeling boxes and bags.

- **Don't skip the orientation programs.** If your child's school offers orientation sessions on move-in day, make it a priority to attend—even if you're sweaty, emotional, and exhausted. Actually, *especially* if you're sweaty, emotional, and exhausted. Still not sold on the idea? Please refer back to chapter 3 to refresh your memory on the value of orientation.

- **Leave 'em with dignity.** Again, once you say good-bye, then head for the door. Red eyes and a few tears are okay, but carrying on for an hour prior to leaving is not helpful for your student.

Remember, your job is to leave your child with a set of twin XL sheets and the confidence that he is equipped for this next stage of life. You've prepared for this day. Your child has the privilege of attending college! If it helps you to let go, think of it as just another summer camp drop-off—without mosquitoes.

EIGHT

CHANGING COURSE AT HOME

I can't control the wind but I can adjust the sail.
—RICKY SKAGGS

As I described in the introduction, every step back to our car on move-in day—not to mention every mile of the five-hour trip home—flooded me with emotion. On that day and in the days that followed, I reflected on the whirlwind of life the past couple of decades.

I had one question: *When did it happen?* I went from college and my first "real" job to marriage and then babies, who grew from toddlers to teens in a nanosecond. A household where diapers, lullabies, and training wheels turned into thongs, indie rock, and driver's ed. Who knew I'd long for the days of chicken nuggets with ketchup? For mismatched socks and tiny shoes? For Legos and Barbies and bedtime stories?

Our daughter's senior year of high school began innocently enough with the subtle undercurrent of change woven throughout the fibers of daily activity. Brooke's senior year kept us busy, and our younger daughter, Karen, and exchange student, Pauline, had many extracurricular activities as well. It all masked reality and allowed me respite from facing what was to come.

Then *it* happened. Brooke donned her cap and gown and to the tune of "Pomp and Circumstance" made me proud and broke my heart at the same time. In the blink of an eye, my baby had gone from diapers to diploma!

I was an emotional wreck inside but didn't have time for a pity party. I had another kind of party to plan. A graduation party. Those party plans kept me occupied and in perpetual denial of the fact that she'd soon leave and life as we knew it would change forever. However, after the party (and it was a *fabulous* party), I had nowhere to hide. It was time to face reality and start packing and planning for her next chapter—and mine.

When Brooke was a tot, she loved me a lot. I mean she *really* loved me and couldn't function unless I was within a four-foot radius of her tiny body. No doors could separate us. Ever. Gone were my days of peeing alone. When I tried to leave the room, she would cling to my leg like a Downy sheet stuck to warm jeans just out of the dryer. I called it love. Dr. Spock called it separation anxiety.

anxiety (noun) a feeling of worry, nervousness, or unease, typically about an imminent event or something with an uncertain outcome.

After spending the better part of two decades immersed in raising our magnificent children, the separation anxiety was now mine. As my gray hairs multiplied, so did my insecurity—my job insecurity. I'd thought of motherhood as my career, my calling. I'd prepared 14,682 kid-friendly meals, listened to 61 school band performances, and applied 377 Band-Aids for both boo-boos and hurt feelings. For heaven's sake, I'd even directed the church Christmas pageant. Twice! Suddenly I was terrified of losing my purpose. I feared that my career (and relevance) would be reduced to an occasional text message and an invitation for parent-and-family weekend. My brain knew it was time for her to separate and assert her independence. But my heart wasn't ready.

For a few days after dropping Brooke off on move-in day, I felt sick. I had no appetite. I was lethargic. I was tired all the time but had a hard time actually sleeping. I went to bed feeling drained and woke up sick to my stomach. As someone who suffers the curse of motion sickness, I can tell you the symptoms were similar. But I hadn't been near a plane, train, or boat. The only trip I'd taken was to Des Moines to drop my baby off at college.

Wait, I suddenly thought one day. *I need to get a grip!* I was confusing motion sickness with emotion sickness. Once I knew emotion sickness was my self-diagnosis, I realized it was up to me to find a cure.

Not every parent gets emotion sickness as I did. And not every parent has the same difficulty letting go. But many still struggle one way or another with the turmoil of conflicting emotions. Sometimes parents who've been challenged by rebellious teens are eager to see their children launch, only to go crazy a few short weeks later because the house is so quiet. Other parents think the transition will be a piece of cake, only to find themselves lonely and obsessing over their child's class schedule, roommate relations, and social life.

No matter what emotions you experience, sending your child off to college is a big change for all family members. Moms, dads, siblings, even grandparents feel a shift. We say good-bye not only to our students but to our familiar, comfortable family routines. What's important is remembering our students are not leaving our families forever. They're just going off to school.

Own Your Grief without Self-Destructing

It's okay to be sad—for a little while. Give yourself some grace. Your child's adjusting to a new way of life, and so are you. But understand this is not an excuse to self-destruct.

Do you think it's a coincidence that parents' midlife crises coincide with their kids' college years? After pouring ourselves into these young humans, we suddenly find ourselves lost in the blind spot of parenting, not sure where we belong or how visible we will be.

While you might want to wrap yourself in a blanket of pity and curl up in Junior's bed surrounded by his stuffed animals and track ribbons, don't do it. Do not allow the dark cloud of desperation to smother you. Instead of reading *Goodnight Moon* until you cry yourself to sleep on a pile of damp Kleenex, think about the amazing opportunities your child is about to experience.

You can own your grief without letting it own you. I'm not saying it's just mind over matter. Trust me—you'll have some undeniably sad moments. They'll creep up on you, like a too-small pair of undies. I'd catch myself tearing up over the most the mundane of daily routines: folding fewer laundry loads, setting only three places at the dinner table instead of our usual four, and walking by her favorite cereal in the grocery aisle.

Seriously, the supermarket is where I had my first—and only—public meltdown a few days after dropping her off at school. I felt the tears bubble up as I passed the dairy section and realized there was no need for me to buy coconut yogurt anymore. Slightly weepy, I started down aisle 7: breads and cereal. As I passed Great Grains Crunchy Pecan cereal, I lost it. I wailed like a foghorn, crying for the little girl with wispy blonde pigtails who no longer existed. I sobbed over the empty bedroom and the hole in my heart and an overpriced box of fiber-filled cereal.

Then I blew my nose and wiped the tears from my now-puffy, crow's-feet-encircled eyes. I put two boxes of Great Grains in my cart. One for the pantry (just because) and one to mail to my little girl.

In case you're wondering, I can now go to the supermarket without Kleenex tucked in my sleeve. It took only a few days to regain my bearings. That old saying about time is spot-on. It can heal a wounded heart—even the heart of a mom who sent her child off to college. It may take a little time to adjust to the new course at home, but with a little TLC and time, you will.

Shifting Currents for Dads

For a few weeks after our firstborn set sail, my husband was not himself. My usually even-keeled partner was distant and often spotted with red, slightly puffy eyes. He was in a funk. When folks sweetly asked how we were doing with Brooke's transition, our younger daughter, Karen, would respond, "Mom and I are okay, but you should see Dad. He's a mess!"

She was right. By that time, I was past the crying-in-public stage and moving toward a new normal. But my husband was still hurting on the inside. He was struggling with his changing role, with letting go. But in his manly fashion, he was not ready to talk about it. Shocker. Mars meet Venus!

Often, men are less likely to talk to friends or partners about how they feel. They may not even admit to themselves that their children's moving out is a big deal. Instead of pouring out his true feelings to anybody with ears, as did his emotional wife, my husband would talk about how great the university was and how excited he was for our girl to be embarking on this grand adventure. He put on a brave face in public and saved his sadness for when he was alone. This closet-softie was just as heartbroken and lost as I was. He just kept it to himself.

Meet Joe, a father of three. His last child to leave the nest chose to attend his alma mater, a large public university six hours from home. At first, he was thrilled his baby girl had the good sense to select this fine institution. After all, he'd had terrific experiences there.

Then reality set in. She'd be six hours from home. This distance meant they'd have no more father-daughter evening runs together. No more weekend bike races. They'd bonded over these events since before she could walk, when he'd push her in a jogging stroller. "I really didn't know how I'd move forward, but I didn't want to ruin the moment for her," he explained.

In typical manly form, he buried his feelings to the outside world. But he did confide in his wife, who was also struggling with the impending empty nest. Together they came up with some ideas for both father and daughter to remain connected over the miles. They could Skype before or after a run. They could "compete" with each other in mileage and track the other's progress with a smartphone app. They ended up buying two sets of sports earbuds with tiny mouthpieces built into the cords so they could jog and chat on the phone at the same time. "It took a little planning to orchestrate our schedules, but we run together from a distance at least once a week," he explains. "It's our special time to catch up."

Rough Passage for Siblings Too

At age two, Brooke wanted a baby sister more than anything in the world. She was over-the-moon excited when we told her we were expecting. Our precocious daughter then informed us the baby would be a girl named Karen. We had no idea where she'd heard the name Karen. We explained to her that we didn't know whether the baby would be a girl or a boy and that mommies and daddies get to pick new babies' names. She didn't buy it. "My baby sister is in my mommy's tummy," she'd tell the people in line behind us at the supermarket. "Her name is Karen."

Eventually, we put the pieces together about where the name Karen came from. Since the beginning of the pregnancy, Brooke had been spending a lot of time in front of her new "babysitter" as daily bouts of morning sickness ravaged my body. Yes, I turned to the device I swore would never replace my love and attention: the television. Each morning while I was tethered to the bathroom, trying not to heave the two-and-a-half saltines I'd just consumed, Brooke happily watched her *Frosty the Snowman* video. Our little TV junkie was enamored with the girl who saved Frosty by getting him on a train to the North Pole—the blonde in the red dress with the earmuffs. The one named Karen.

Brooke was relentless over the next several months, continuing to insist her baby would be a girl named Karen. And naturally, Karen would like to play Barbies. We maintained our position as name givers and wondered what she'd do if her baby came out a boy. We tried to prepare her for reality, introducing other names such as Jordan and Kyle and Brett.

After a relatively short labor that culminated in a "challenging" delivery, we had a healthy baby. My proud husband was elated. He jumped up and down in the hospital room repeating, "It's a Karen! It's a Karen!"

From the day Karen came into this world, she and Brooke were two peas in a pod. Both blue-eyed blondes. Both born in May. Both spirited. Even though Brooke was a bit disappointed that her newborn sister didn't show an immediate interest in Barbies, she was Karen's biggest fan and cheerleader. Brooke wore her "I'm the Big Sister" T-shirt until it was threadbare and two sizes too small. As years passed, the girls even began to look alike. Despite their being three years and two weeks apart in age, I was often asked if they were twins.

Karen followed her big sister around and mimicked her every move. If Brooke did something, Karen was a single step behind with an enthusiastic "Me too! Me too!" It didn't matter what Brooke did, her little sister was there with a "Me too!" If Brooke wanted to read a book, she heard, "Me too!" If she chose to eat Goldfish crackers for a snack, "Me too!" Go to the potty? "Me too!" Our friends began calling them "Me" and "Me-Too."

But as Me and Me-Too continued to grow, separation was inevitable. My mom-heart ripped in two when we watched Brooke climb up the steps into the big yellow school bus on the first day of kindergarten. I remember Me-Too waiting, her little chin resting on the window ledge and nose pressed against the glass, for her big sister to return home every afternoon.

But they adjusted. They figured out how to make the most of the time they did have together. As the years passed, they continued to stay close despite the three years that separated them. They played Barbies in their younger years and played on the same tennis team through junior high and high school. They shared sweaters, shoes, and secrets.

When Me began her senior year, Me-Too was a freshman at the same high school. Her big sister kept a watchful eye out for her. They drove to school together in the morning and studied together at night.

That year, I began to worry about how "The Day" would affect Me-Too. No matter how many times I pushed the thought out of my mind, the questions came: How would they stay in touch? How would they maintain the laughter and chatter and secrets with 321 miles between them? How could I help prepare Me-Too for the flood of emotions I knew she'd feel as she watched her sidekick load up her belongings and move away?

"The Day" came. Me-Too had a tennis tournament and couldn't join us in moving her sister to college. Was her absence a blessing or a curse? Was it easier to part this way—or more difficult?

Me-Too is a tough one, private with her emotions. My maternal intuition told me she was struggling that first week alone. While her sister was consumed with the busyness of her new college life, Me-Too was trying to adapt to her newfound only-child-at-home status. To put it in her words, "It was rough."

One night I found her, with tear-stained cheeks, snuggled in her sister's bed. And the worst part? I couldn't fix it. She was lonely and had to figure out her new identity as an only child, the one left behind. I was shocked by the depth of her hurt. She pulled away from us and spent a lot of time alone in her room. Her life was turned upside down, and only she could figure out how to move on. We couldn't do it for her.

As days turned to weeks and the new school year began, life moved on for Me-Too too. She became busy with tennis and classes.

And once again, these two sisters adjusted. Just as they had when Brooke left for kindergarten, they figured out how to overcome this new separation. One day, I heard Karen giggling downstairs. She was talking to her sister screen-to-screen. Thanks to technology, our girls were as close as ever, talking, texting, and Snapchatting several times a day. They were quick to FaceTime each other for fashion advice and to share the latest news. Sometimes they even watched their favorite shows together. It wasn't the same as being face-to-face, but it made the transition much easier and made 321 miles not seem so far away.

Since those first rough weeks, Karen has matured and evolved and adjusted to her new role. Instead of hearing, "Hey, aren't you Brooke's little sister?" on a regular basis at school, she's now Karen. Just Karen. At home, she shoulders more responsibilities as the-one-left-behind-to-make-Mom-and-Dad-feel-needed. Of course, she takes advantage of every opportunity to use the car. She drives her dad to their favorite coffee shop on Saturday mornings and picks up groceries on her way home from the gym. She and her friends bring life and laughter and Chinese takeout into our too-quiet home.

Karen's become more independent, more confident. She still misses her sister and looks forward to every in-person and on-screen chat. But she has survived and is now starting her own college search—looking at colleges sixteen hundred miles from home. Time for this mom to get her own Snapchat account!

When your own college student launches, your family dynamics will change too. It is inevitable. Please remember that siblings still living at home will go through a transformation as well.

Just as you may be processing conflicting emotions, so may your other children. Some siblings are happy to move up the pecking order and reap such benefits as more access to the car. Others are eager to take over their older sib's bedroom. Some are indifferent, too busy with their own lives to feel a strong impact. Yet others, like our younger daughter, will struggle with some sadness or loss as they adjust to the new normal at home. No matter where your younger children fall on this spectrum, be sensitive to their feelings. Remember it is okay for them to not miss an older sibling, just as it's okay to really miss one.

If your child appears indifferent or even happy to see his older sib go, don't worry. It's not necessarily a reflection of their relationship or even your parenting. Keep in mind that so much attention has been focused on that older sibling for the past several months. Your younger child may see this is a chance to get more of your attention—and not have to share the bathroom.

Obviously, how you address this change with your children will depend on their ages as well as your family dynamics. A high school–aged sibling will have different perceptions and needs than a younger child. Here are some ideas that may help your children through this transition:

- Encourage your child at home to reach out to her older sibling through social media, e-mail, phone calls, or texts. A much younger sibling can draw pictures or write letters you can send via snail mail.

- Allow the younger sibling to assemble and mail a care package. For creative care package ideas, see chapter 9 and the appendix.

- Encourage your college student to stay in touch with his younger sibling. Ask him to make time each week to connect.

- Plan to attend parent-and-family weekend or schedule a sibling visit (if possible).

- Remind your remaining children that their older sibling is still a part of the family—no matter where he lives. Also, in a few weeks or months, that older sibling will return for breaks—so they should be prepared to go back to sharing. You'll find more on that readjustment stage in chapter 14.

Stay on Course

Sending your child off to college is a little like taking a young family on a big vacation. It's both stressful and exciting. It requires careful planning and attention to detail. (And lots of money.)

You spend a considerable amount of time researching the

destination and planning kid-friendly itineraries. You make packing lists and buy appropriate clothing. You prepare the kids by reading books together and talking about what to expect at the airport. You tuck ample snacks and activities in their little rolling suitcases to occupy them on the flight.

When you're all buckled safely into your seats, you realize you forgot to use the restroom yourself when you took the kids prior to boarding. And then the flight attendants begin the safety presentation, including the part about oxygen masks dropping from the panel above in the event of cabin depressurization. They remind you, "If you are traveling with a child or someone who requires assistance, secure your mask first, then assist the other person."

In other words, you're no good to your family if you can't take care of yourself. This same theory applies to launching your kids on the college voyage. This trip requires lots of time, energy, and planning too. It can take its toll on even the strongest parents. But just remember: you can't properly support your student if you're depleted and not caring for yourself.

You can find lots of well-intended articles on self-care and stress reduction. I'm always amazed at the suggestions. Get a hot $tone ma$$age. Treat yourself to a $pa pedicure. Or better yet, an entire $pa day. Make a re$ervation at your favorite four-$tar restaurant. Join a health club and take a hot yoga cla$$.

Reality check: college is expen$ive. These stress-busters may be nice—if we weren't helping pay for tuition and fees (and phones and gas and insurance). And really, must we break our budgets to take care of ourselves? Does throwing money at our problems actually make them go away?

In lieu of spending a small fortune on self-care, here are a few methods I've found helpful to take care of myself as I manage this life-changing transition:

Focus on Family and Friends

One of my favorite Beatles' songs reveals the secret to how I survived my daughter's launch: *I get by with a little help from my friends.* I honestly don't know how I would have survived without the help of my girlfriends—my tribe, my village. A few friends had already launched their kids, and others were in the thick of it, like me. I was amazed at how many women sent a quick "How are you?" in the weeks that followed "The Day." My tribe was there for me, and it made all the difference in the world.

Cultivate your connections. Learn from friends who have survived this experience, and commiserate with those facing the same struggles. Lean on your friends and family now, and look forward to the day when you can be part of a support system for others.

Pay Extra Attention to Your Partner

It's very common for partners to have anxiety when their kids move out—especially those facing an empty nest. With the kids gone, what will we talk about? Will we get sick of each other's company? Do we still have enough in common? If these questions are floating around in your head, please know there's hope! In fact, some studies show that marital happiness actually increases after the kids leave home.

When your student leaves for college, you and your partner will want to put a little extra effort into each other. Start by talking—but not about the kids or work or bills. Instead, talk about all the benefits of having the house to yourselves. What are you each looking forward to? More free time? Traveling? Eating out at new restaurants? Fewer loads of laundry? Skinny-dipping in your pool? Freedom to try a new hobby? Don't just sit back and fixate on your quiet house. Start dating each other again! Try a new restaurant. Sign up for a couples' bowling league. Start a neighborhood card club.

Remember when your kids were little and you lamented the loss of spontaneity and romance? Now's the time to bring a little romance back into your nest. One of the best ways to get out of a relationship rut (and dare I say ignite passion) is to shake up your normal routine. For example, in the evening, instead of retiring to separate ends of the couch with your own phone or tablet or book, get cozy and watch a movie together while giving each other foot massages. Take a sunset stroll or uncork a good bottle of wine—on a Tuesday night, just because you can. Even the smallest changes and surprises can help keep a relationship fresh and exciting and help remind you that there are benefits to this time of transition.

Put It on Paper

Maybe it's the writer in me, but I find journaling to be a particularly helpful outlet. No, I'm not telling you to author a book! But when I have the urge to call my daughter for the third time in a day, I sit down instead and write what I want to share with her. I can list my joys, concerns, fears, dreams, and prayer requests. Somehow, I gain a sense of perspective by writing things down on paper. My journal is a place where I can commemorate details and release anxiety.

I also use my journal as a place to jot down inspirational quotes or Bible verses I can send Brooke later via snail mail. Sometimes it helps me feel connected to write and mail a short uplifting note to her, and my journal is the perfect place to gather ideas. (See chapter 9 for more details about sending your love through the mail.)

Meditate or Pray

Jan is convinced meditation got her through her only child's move halfway across the country. She joined a weekly meditation group that centers her.

If you're new to meditation, just know there's no wrong way to do it. You can find several suggested practices with a simple Google search.

For instance, you can start by getting comfortable and closing your eyes. Breathe deeply. Think about your child and all the positive college experiences he may encounter. Focus on the good, and imagine your student in healthy, enlightening situations. Paint a picture in your mind, and keep breathing. Your imagination will help reduce the negative images and reinforce the positive ones.

Personally, I found that prayer—another form of meditation—brought me comfort. Somehow prayer grounds me and allows me to receive some divine perspective for my irrational maternal fears.

Whether it's meditation, prayer, or some other centering practice, just figure out what works to help you find balance during this time of change.

Exercise

It may seem cliché, I know. But exercise really does help pull parents out of an I'm-missing-my-baby funk. To quote Elle Woods from *Legally Blonde* (incidentally, one of our girls' favorite movies): "Exercise gives you endorphins. Endorphins make you happy. Happy people just don't shoot their husbands. They just don't." While I don't intend to mock murder, you get the point on endorphins and happy people. For our purposes, let's change the quote to, "Exercise gives you endorphins. Endorphins make you happy. Happy people learn to function again after their children leave for college."

So get out there! Take a hike, dust off your tennis racket, or sign up for a Zumba class. Sweat out that anxiety. Do this for yourself—and for your child. It's another way you can model healthy behavior.

Wine—Don't Whine

All right—as long as I'm reflecting on my coping skills, I might as well be honest. When I feel like whining about missing my little girl, sometimes I put on my flannel snowflake pajamas, pour a big glass of a rich red zin, and watch *Big Bang Theory* reruns instead. While expressing emotions is healthy, incessantly whining and rehashing negatives isn't. In this case, a room temperature goblet of relaxation accompanied with some ridiculous humor seems to soothe my soul. Plus, Sheldon Cooper's antics make my many quirks seem so much less severe.

You Will Survive

There are many techniques to help you adapt to the new normal in your household. In truth, most parents find the transition gets easier over time—as they see their children settle in and thrive in their new environments.

But even as time passes, I often wonder if the bittersweet emotions of letting go will ever entirely disappear. Are they simply a part of parenthood? Are they gentle reminders of the depth of the bonds we have with our children?

At the beginning of this book, I promised you *real* information from someone who has bobbed over these sometimes-stormy seas—someone who truly understands the tsunami of mixed emotions churning in your head (and heart) right now. Believe me—I understand. I'm the mom who bawled through *Toy Story 3* as Andy prepared to leave for college. I sopped up my elephant tears with Kleenex as Andy and his mom said their good-byes in his nearly empty childhood bedroom.

Mom: "I wish I could always be with you."

Andy: "You will be, Mom."

Those lines nearly did me in! No matter how old they get and no matter how far they go, they will always be our babies.

While I can't tell you it will always be smooth sailing, I can guarantee you're about to embark on an adventure of a lifetime. Both you and your student will stretch yourselves as you transition into a new normal. You may not be there tucking him into his twin extra-long bed each night, but your loving support and the life skills and the values you've instilled will be. Always.

Your primal urge to protect will never disappear, but you'll learn when to back off and empower your child to make decisions (hopefully smart, healthy ones) and take responsibility for her own well-being. It's both thrilling and terrifying to watch your child transition into adulthood.

While this year will be an exercise in letting go, please understand that you are not obsolete! Your child will still need you to mentor and guide, to model emotionally healthy behavior. You're still a soft place to land, an anchor, and a sounding board when situations come up that he's not ready handle. Be there. Listen. Show compassion when insecurities bubble to the surface—both yours and his.

This moment comes along once in a lifetime. Embrace this opportunity to provide support and love. Then, let go. Step back and watch your child set sail.

You will survive. I promise.

NINE

SHIP-TO-SHORE COMMUNICATION

*We are like islands in the sea, separate on the surface
but connected in the deep.*
—WILLIAM JAMES

The most practical advice we received about the freshman voyage came from one of the dads on the advisory panel at our parent-orientation session. Wearing his "Drake Dad" baseball cap, he beamed with pride as he shared tales of his two daughters: one an alumna with a paying job in her field (music to the ears of every parent in the room) and the other a senior with a double major in journalism and prelaw.

The dad began with the basics of move-in day. He encouraged everyone to bring a rubber mallet to aid in lofting the beds. He lauded the versatility of 3M Command strips and extra-long TV cables. He warned us about the hidden fees on particular ATM cards.

Then he dropped the bomb: he told us we needed to lower our

expectations. To the confused sea of faces staring at him, he clarified, "However much you expect your child will call you or e-mail you, lower your expectations by at least half."

Mary, a petite panelist with a sophomore son, chimed in. When Jared left for school, she assumed they'd text daily and talk a couple of times a week. But after two weeks of zero contact, she was more worried than irritated. When she did finally get her son on the other end of the phone, she was shocked to learn Jared had been so busy with classes, band, and his newfound social life that he simply "forgot" to call his mother.

She recognized that he was happy and enjoying his newfound freedom. But she also made it clear that he did, in fact, need to call home at least once a week to check in. And like any good mother, she followed it up with a threat and a healthy dose of guilt. She let him know if he "forgot" to call again, she would simply show up at his door with her overnight bag in hand. Funny thing—he always remembered to call after that.

What expectations do you have for texting and chatting with your student? Are you prepared to take the Drake dad's advice about cutting it in half? What are the best ways to reach your child? Let's explore these questions and more.

Setting Reasonable Expectations—Together

Parents must remember this is college. It will look and feel different than high school. Communication from your student may ebb and flow. There may be periods of radio silence.

"In a world where people are available by cell phone and text all the time, parents get concerned when their students (often for the first time) don't text or call back immediately," explains Dr. Cara Halgren, UND associate vice president and dean of students.

Of course, there's nothing wrong with parents checking in now and then. Moms and dads need a little reassurance too. We make many adjustments when our children go off to college. But one thing that doesn't change is our worry. We worry about safety, health, roommates, and coed dorm floors. It's easy to treat the sound of our student's voice or the sight of a text as an elixir for that worry.

But do you really need to text or talk to your child every day? Is it for *her* benefit? Or is it because you're unwilling to let go? Does he call you? Or are you always doing the calling? We parents obviously know our own children best. But we can also get so wrapped up in missing them that we can't see the negative impact of excessive contact.

These are just some of the issues that came up when discussing this hot topic with a group of parents. In our informal poll, opinions varied on how often to expect contact. But all were in agreement that the student should usually initiate contact.

If you're like Mary and don't hear from your student as often as you'd like, take it as a good sign. No news is usually good news. He's likely happy, healthy, and actively engaged in university life. Your child will be in touch when he needs something or has exciting news to share. Or he'll call when he's bored and walking across campus, as my daughter does.

If you're concerned about the lines of communication, then *communicate* that. As Dr. Halgren states, "I encourage parents to talk with their students about developing an agreed upon 'reasonable' response."

In other words, take time to discuss your expectations—but with the understanding that your child may need to pull away a bit in order to fully engage in college life. Together, set some agreed-upon rules about how and when you'll stay in touch. Ideally, you should do this before move-in day, but if you're past that point, there's no time like the present.

It takes open and honest conversation to set boundaries both students and parents can agree upon. According to Dr. Halgren, having these frank conversations and setting concrete expectations ahead of time prevents unnecessary parental anxiety while allowing students to grow up and develop autonomy.

For some families, healthy contact may mean a daily text. For others, it may be a weekend family Skype session. You may agree to not contact your child more than once per week. Or she may want to schedule a biweekly chat time. You may suggest your child initiate contact at her convenience.

Letting Go of the Electronic Leash

I think back to the middle school years, when our daughters began their quest for cell phones. Our poor, cell phone–deprived daughters bemoaned the challenges of being phoneless. They campaigned day and night, illustrating how much a cell phone would improve their lives.

"Really, Mom," one of them posited, "I'll get better grades because I can call my friends when I have algebra questions you can't help me with." *As if I had actually ever been able to help her with algebra.* "I'll never be late for school because phones also have alarm clocks on them." *As if a phone would actually push her out of bed in the morning.*

Call me old-fashioned. Call me cheap. Call me Mom. Back then, I wasn't ready for my children to possess that much technology.

Of course, time wore on. Eventually, we did allow them to acquire cell phones of their own. But only because we could use the phones as yet another opportunity to teach the girls about privileges and responsibilities. And because we could use the phones as electronic leashes.

You see, that's how I grew to view those little plastic gadgets. My theory was, if I called, they had to answer immediately, like a tug on the leash. They didn't have the luxury of ignoring me and calling back later. I saw this as a safety thing and a mom thing— and to be brutally honest, a control thing for a parent who wasn't thrilled at the thought of her daughters growing up and pulling away. Please don't judge me too harshly. In this big, scary world, I wanted to know they were okay when they weren't under our roof.

While the electronic leash philosophy may have worked effectively in a middle school setting, it is neither effective nor necessary in college. By the time children leave for college, they've hopefully developed the ability to survive without reporting every hiccup or test score back to Mama. And hopefully Mama too has developed the ability to survive without 24-7 access.

"The important thing is that the student feels respected and not restricted by your contact," says a mom of two boys, both in college. "We raise our kids to be successful, independent adults. Does demanding a phone call every day express love? Or does it tell them we're still micromanaging their lives?" Another mom asks, "Isn't this what we just spent the last eighteen years preparing them for?"

Gracefully and gradually, we must learn to be quieter, to give fewer answers, and to ask more questions. Now is the time to model emotionally healthy behavior for your child. Letting go of the electronic leash is one such way.

Cell Phones as Safety

That all said, let's return back to the concept of a cell phone as a safety measure. No, it's not middle school anymore. You can't force your college student to drop everything and reply immediately whenever you call or text. But it's still a big, scary world, and a cell phone can still be a form of security.

As you and your student discuss your agreed-upon expectations about communication, don't forget to address this scenario: Say you, like Mary, contact your student and wait for a reply. And wait. And wait some more. What do you do when your contact goes unanswered—for days? Nothing fuels worry like not getting a reply as simple proof of life.

As in the case with Mary's son, not hearing back from your student likely means he's having the time of his life. Or maybe not. Let's be honest—scary things *do* happen on campus. (See chapter 13.) Not returning texts or calls could be a warning sign to not dismiss.

For your child's well-being and your peace of mind, you may wish to set up a safety protocol. For example, perhaps you'll agree that your student will respond within twenty-four hours after you make contact. A simple "Got it—will reply later" will do if he's too busy for a long call or detailed text. But if you don't hear *anything* back within twenty-four hours, you'll choose to contact campus safety for a personal welfare check.

Again, having this "reasonable response" protocol in place and setting these expectations saves parents from anxiety while allowing students to grow up and develop autonomy.

Texting Temptations

I think I can speak for many parents when I say I'd much rather pick up the phone and call my babies instead of plunking out a text. On a phone call, I can discern their well-being simply by hearing them speak. We all developed this parental radar when they were infants. It allowed us to immediately interpret which cry meant "I'm hungry" and which one meant "I've loaded up my pants and need a little help here." Now this radar enables us to decipher "I'm lonely" or "My girlfriend dumped me" or, music to our ears, "I miss your meat loaf, Mom."

But while we may prefer phone calls or face-to-face visits, our technology-savvy kids have lightning-fast thumbs and often prefer to text. They like convenience. They like control. They like immediate gratification. With texting, they choose when a conversation starts and how long it lasts. They can pop off a text between classes or during class. They can connect on their terms and their schedule.

So, to speak their language, we parents need to embrace texting—the key, I think, to twenty-first-century kid-to-parent communication. Our job now is to listen, to be mentors and anchors. Making ourselves available via texting is one way to reach out. If texting keeps the lines of communication open, it's worth putting up with some thumb gymnastics, isn't it?

I may be encouraging texting as a communication tool, but please know I'm not suggesting overwhelming your child with dozens of daily texts. With smartphones at our fingertips, texting temptation is ever present. But too much of a good thing is no good.

In spite of our parental desire to connect with our offspring daily (or more often), experts suggest the same philosophy that applies to telephone contact applies to texting as well. Allow your child to make the first move, and set agreed-upon expectations up front.

Face-to-Face Contact

Thanks to today's technology, we now can have face-to-face contact with our children from across the country or across the pond. Skype, FaceTime, and other similar video chatting apps allow us to see our cherubs via computer or smartphone anytime day or night. For those of you older than me, this is like video conferencing. For those of you younger and more tech-savvy than me, feel free to skip this section. You already know this stuff.

Many parents and students find this face-to-face contact a great way to connect. Video chatting is the next best thing to actually being right there in person together. One first-year student fighting a bout of homesickness said Skype was just the medicine she needed to work through it. Seeing her puppy was all it took to get her back on track.

My daughter's roommate was seven hundred miles from home in Colorado. The oldest of four children, she was concerned about missing her younger siblings' milestones and afraid they'd forget her while she was gone. I asked her to share her thoughts on staying connected over the miles via Skype.

> *I always set aside an hour or so on Sunday afternoons to talk to my family. It allows me not only to catch up with them verbally but also to show them what I'm up to. They've been able to see my dorm room, roommates, friends, art projects, and even what I'm having for dinner in real time, which helps bridge the distance gap.*
>
> *I have found that Skype helps me catch up with my younger siblings more effectively than just a phone call. I can see their expressions and body language. Sometimes they get distracted by seeing their own faces on the screen, but most of the time their answers are more genuine because it's face-to-face.*
>
> *During freshman year it was easy for me to think of my college life in Des Moines as totally and completely separate from my home life in Colorado, which was not what I wanted to be the case. Since my parents weren't able to come out and visit me last year, Skyping them every week really helped bridge the gap.*

As my daughter's roommate explained, video chatting is a great way to "see" life inside the dorm. You can meet your child's roommate and friends and connect faces with names. Unfortunately, it also gives you a chance to see his housekeeping skills. Don't be surprised if in the background you see an unmade bed and three weeks' worth of dirty laundry strewn about the floor. Such is college life.

For the best video chatting experience:

1. Plan ahead and set a time so you're both prepared to chat.

2. Don't multitask. Your child wants to see your eyes and feel your love, not watch you wash dishes.

3. Try to eliminate background noise so she can hear your voice. She didn't call to listen to the football game. (Unless, of course, the football game is the reason you're video chatting. My daughters often watch TV together via FaceTime.)

4. Make sure you have a good Internet connection, or you'll spend more time looking at a frozen screen than talking with your child.

5. Be patient. Technology is terrific—when it works.

6. *Wear clothes.* Remember, whoever walks into your child's dorm room can see you too. No girl wants her roommate to see Dad in his boxers.

E-mail: Another Survival Tool

E-mail can be another communication tool in your fresh-man-year-survival toolbox. Some people (mostly parents) access e-mail from a computer at specific times of the day. Other people receive and send e-mails from their smartphones, making e-mail as mobile as texting.

However, my daughter assures me e-mail is going the way of the telegraph. She says students much prefer texting or even calling. Parents, though, still view e-mail as a casual, less-intense method for sharing quick bits of information with their children. For our generation, e-mail bridges today's texting and yesterday's letter writing. One dad told me he doesn't take the time to pen a handwritten letter but can quickly send off a short e-mail from the office. (More on handwritten letters later in the chapter.)

And while texting may be the norm on campus, some students actually prefer e-mail contact from home. "I find it less intrusive to e-mail," says Anna. "As a junior, I'm much busier between classes and work, so I don't have a lot of time to hang out on the phone." She continues, "We still communicate, but at times of day that are more convenient for both my parents and me."

Many families find e-mail especially useful for handling the business end of college life. A question about medical insurance coverage, for example, can be taken care of efficiently and conveniently via e-mail (as long as it isn't sent from the ER at 3:00 a.m.).

Instant Communication: A Blessing and a Curse

Ever-evolving technology has drastically affected relation-ships between students and parents. The speed in which we can connect today is remarkable. However, this technology can be both a blessing and a curse. The blessing? More communication than ever between students and parents. The curse? Knee-jerk reactions.

Due to the speed of communication, today's students do not spend much time actually processing information for themselves before phoning home or sending off an intense e-mail or text message. Parents hear about a conflict or a struggle while it is still raw and emotional and possessing a sense of urgency.

Expect these instant reactions to roll in about a month into the school year. By that point, the newness of college has worn off, and your child has figured out some things for herself. She might now realize the crazy life-of-the-party friend she met the first week is actually shallow and irritating. She'll start to think the fun guys next door with the amazing stereo might not be so cool when their bass is thumping through the walls at 4:00 a.m. The service club she joined might require a greater time commitment than she first expected. And the moment she figures these things out, you can expect a call or a text, no matter what time of day.

Whether it's a tearful call about the first C on a paper or an annoying roommate's actions, parents often hear news within minutes—before the student has had a chance to think things through. What might actually be a minor situation comes across as a major crisis. Instead of processing the problem and coming up with courses of action on their own, kids immediately call Mom and Dad to vent. In turn, parental instinct kicks in, and we take on the role of fixer, not mentor.

A poignant example of this occurred a few years ago, when Jada was on a six-month study abroad program in France. One evening on her way to night class, she misread the transportation schedule and subsequently missed her connecting bus. Standing alone in the dark bus station, frustrated and knowing she'd be late to class at the university, Jada did the first thing that came to her mind. She pulled her cell phone from her backpack and called her mom—in North Dakota. Not the professor. Not the university. Not a cab.

Like most kids of this generation, Jada's instincts were to call her parent. Immediately. While this provides job security for moms and dads everywhere, it also illustrates how the availability of instant cell phone communication has impaired some of the critical-thinking and problem-solving skills necessary in life.

What would Jada have done without a cell phone in her pocket—say, if this had happened fifteen years ago? Would she have used her fluent French to talk to a passerby about alternative transportation? Would she have found a pay phone to contact the university? (She certainly wouldn't waste her money calling her mother long distance.)

On the other end of the line, what's a parent to do when your daughter calls you and dumps the latest drama du jour on your plate? You know the kind of call . . .

"Like, Dad, I have a ten-page research paper and fifty hours of calculus due, and I haven't slept in three weeks, and I'll have to drop out of college if I don't get it all done by tomorrow. What should I do?"

Hmm. How to react to this supersized serving of emotion? How *not* to react?

When faced with such dire straits from our daughter, my husband responds with this simple question: "Honey, how do you eat an elephant?"

Then, following an Oscar-worthy sigh, she'll respond, "I know, Dad—one bite at a time."

Do you remember Alison's anchor theory from chapter one? These knee-jerk phone calls are terrific times to apply it. Just like seven-year-olds, college students may occasionally need to touch base with their parents (a source of security) for reassurance.

They're not looking for advice or lectures, just anchors.

So the next time you get one of "those" calls—when your child dumps all his worries, fears, and anxieties on you—take pause. Ask yourself if he's really in trouble or if he just needs to anchor. After you listen as a mentor and encourage him to find his own solutions, you can hang up the phone and celebrate the fact that your child turned to you. You are a trusted source of security and comfort. You are providing both anchors and sails.

The Power of the Written Word

When our girls were younger, I'd slip notes (usually with quotes) in their lunch boxes or sport bags. If they were heading on a church trip or long weekend, I'd hide one in their duffel bags. On occasion, I even used a Sharpie to write a message on a banana. Today, I send little cards and notes to Brooke in the mail.

In a culture of lightning-fast texting and e-mail, is a handwritten letter old-fashioned? Maybe. But who doesn't like a little note of affirmation to brighten her day? Imagine your jig of joy if you opened your mailbox and found a simple note of gratitude or encouragement instead of a pile of bills.

Texting is efficient when you're short on time but still want to connect. It's an instantaneous way to say, "I'm thinking about you" or "Yes, I deposited $$ into your account." But if you want to make a larger impact, do not underestimate the power of the handwritten letter. I'm a firm believer in the virtue of snail mail, especially when the message is positive and intentional. By intentional, I mean with the purpose of building someone up and affirming the best qualities of his character.

I know this will sound like a writing assignment for English 101, so please don't be scared off by this suggestion: Grab a piece of paper. Any paper will do. It can be a greeting card, personalized stationary, a basic piece of white printer paper, or the back of a cocktail napkin. It's not about how fancy your paper is. It's about the message you'll write on it. Next, think about your precious off-spring. What parts of his character make you proud? What personality traits make you smile? What would you really like him to know?

Dig a little deeper than the typical "Have a nice day" or "Hope you're having fun." Think of words that inspire, comfort, support, and show you "get" him. Note some of his positive attributes and elaborate on how valuable those qualities are in life. For example, "I've always admired your enthusiasm for helping others. I know this will open doors for you and help you meet other kind-hearted people."

In case you are stuck, turn to a thesaurus or refer to the appendix in the back of the book for inspiration. Hunt for words that go beyond *nice* to describe deeper character qualities worth recognizing.

If you've looked at the words in the appendix and you're still staring at that paper at a loss for words, try a motivational quote. That's often a good place to start. Find one that speaks to you, and jot it down on that napkin, followed by a few sentences about why you like the quote. A simple Google search or trip to the bookstore or library will generate plenty of quotes. There are also some in the appendix.

Lastly, add a few more sentences of encouragement and praise and—voilà!—you've got a day-brightening note to pop in the mailbox. Get creative as you'd like with these little notes. (Although I don't recommend mailing bananas.)

Care Package 101

Last spring, I had the privilege of sitting down with a group of experienced RAs at a large northwest university. I asked them what was the best way to boost a first-year student's morale. They all agreed care packages are the ticket to happiness—sunshine on a cloudy day. "Kids want care packages," admitted Allie, a junior. Who knew there could be such power in a shoe box?

Plenty of online companies specialize in sending college care packages. It's a nice option for folks who want convenience. Some schools even sell and deliver care packages as a fundraiser, sending order forms to parents prior to finals week. Personally, I actually enjoyed putting them together myself. (More on this below.) Whether they're handmade or custom ordered, please know packages don't have to cost a small fortune. In fact, if you're doing it yourself, the dollar store is a great place to start.

If you're sending homemade goodies, be sure to send enough for your child to share with friends. However, I encourage you to think beyond the cookie. Please don't get me wrong—I'm not anti-cookie. I actually really like cookies. And I know college students love cookies, especially Mom's cookies. I just happen to think we can send more sunshine with a little extra creativity.

Plus, I remember my own college years, when I thoroughly enjoyed all the treats my mom, grandmas, and aunts sent me. I also enjoyed the midnight pizzas, french fry study sessions, and the conveniently located frozen yogurt shop. I gained my freshman fifteen, then my sophomore seventeen. I jiggled from my junior twenty. You get the point. It took years to lose the weight I added in college.

So, when creating care packages, I do my best to include some low-cal (or no-cal) items along with the occasional homemade cookies. To help inspire your own creativity, I've compiled a list of care package ideas in the appendix. You'll find ideas for major milestones and year-round themes—everything from "Birthday Party in a Box" to "Finals Survival Kit." So stock up on bubble wrap and get started!

LEARNING THE ROPES

Thought is the wind, knowledge the sail,
and mankind the vessel.
—AUGUSTUS HARE

Grant was a superstar in his suburban high school—popular, athletic, academically gifted. He graduated with honors and followed his dream of attending a Big Ten college several hours from home.

Then at Thanksgiving break, Grant let it slip that he was struggling academically. When his parents prodded, he admitted was failing all but one of his classes. Not only had he underestimated the difficulty of his courses but he also hadn't appropriately managed his newfound freedom. He got caught up in the party scene and often slept through his classes, which clearly impacted his grades.

His parents were shocked. How could this be? What had happened? And why hadn't the university contacted them to let them know there was a problem?

Whether they struggle or shine at college, hopefully your children will be eager to share their academic experiences with you. Because that, my friends, is the only way you'll learn of your student's successes and failures. Let me restate that: if you want to know your child's academic scores, you will have to hear it from him. You won't get report cards. You can't log in to the school website to check for missing assignments. This is college.

Believe it or not, in the eyes of the university, your child is an adult. Her business is no longer your business. I realize this doesn't seem fair. Most likely, you're helping foot the bill. Plus, you birthed this young human. You fed her. You raised her. You dropped her off at college just a few weeks ago. So why can't you see how she's doing in school?

While I personally believe your fading stretch marks and diminishing savings account validate your desire to see Junior's collegiate report cards, the Family Educational Rights and Privacy Act (FERPA) says otherwise. FERPA is a federal law that protects the privacy of student education records, including grades, transcripts, test scores, disciplinary records, financial records, and class schedules.

Like it or not, this is yet another leg of the voyage that forces us to step back and allow our students to navigate uncharted waters on their own. Our students will be making their own decisions when registering for class and declaring majors. Some may change majors multiple times. Others will not waver. Some will struggle with grades. Others will sail through with nary a worry. But they will do it without any formal involvement from you.

Maybe you feel confident in your child's ability to step up to this new responsibility. But if you're concerned about him making poor decisions or making his undergrad program the best six, seven, or eight years of his life, grab your mentor hat and place it firmly on your head.

Respectfully share your concerns. Ask questions. Reinforce your relationship with open, supportive conversation about the long-term impact of academic choices. And keep in mind he's teetering on the cusp of adult life—learning the ropes as he goes.

Classes and Registration

In high school, some parents help their children select classes. Usually, it's a fairly anticlimactic process, with decisions vacillating between regular bio and AP bio. But in college, choosing classes falls solely on your child's shoulders, and the options are considerably more liberating—and nerve-racking, especially for first-year students.

If you're tempted to step in and help with (i.e., micromanage) your child's schedule, please don't. This is an opportunity for letting her figure out a challenging situation and apply decision-making skills. In fact, she probably registered for her first semester classes without your even realizing it. Depending on the university, incoming freshmen often choose their courses during orientation, before school begins—without a parent in sight.

Universities understand registering for classes can be overwhelming for first-year students. They have trained staff—such as the academic advisors we met in chapter 3—to assist your student through the process. Your child will be encouraged to take on a challenging but reasonable workload, especially for the first semester. This will allow time to make a smoother, less stressful transition into college.

As freshmen, students select classes that fulfill their general education requirements. Translation? Before they can graduate, they must take a certain number of courses in communication arts, math, humanities, social sciences, sciences, and liberal arts. The general education requirements lay the foundation for their degree programs, when their courses will focus much more on their chosen majors or fields.

So don't be surprised if your child is taking a class on an obscure topic you've never even thought about. Many parents struggle to see the necessity of general education courses that don't seemingly line up with specific career goals. Why does she need to take a foreign language when she's going into engineering? What does art history have to do with nursing? Why are we paying for those classes, anyway?

Parents, keep in mind this is the "well-rounded" component of your child's education—the part that broadens her scope of learning and enriches her life. This is the time in her life to try something new. If you attended a four-year college yourself, think back to the variety of classes you took. Plus, if your student has an undecided major, those general classes may help her identify an area of interest.

It's also important to realize that our children will likely have several jobs in their futures. Today's technological advances, combined with the global marketplace, make our children's career paths quite different from our parents' or our own. Our kids won't hold the same position for a lifetime. They may even hold jobs that aren't yet in existence as they register for their first-year classes. In other words, you never know when that art history class will come in handy, so it's important to step back and allow your student to explore these new waters on her own.

That said, it's vital your student knows that selecting appropriate classes helps her graduate on time and gets her the most bang for the collegiate buck. Let's take a closer look, then, at how each class brings your student closer to—or farther from—her goals.

Setting the Four-Year Course

If you crunched numbers with your student after reading chapter 4, then hopefully your child understands the value of setting course for graduating in four years. We've already discussed this from a financial perspective. Now let's discuss it from an academic angle. Careful planning is paramount in getting the job done in four years, and it begins right away—during the freshman year.

Let's assume time and money are relevant to families of college students. As explained in chapter 4, most parents have solid expectations that their students will earn undergraduate degrees in four years. While this is an attainable and desirable goal, it's not a gimme. According to the *Four-Year Myth* study by Complete College America in 2014, only 19 percent of students attending public universities actually graduate in four years. At flagship or research universities, it's only 36 percent of full-time students.

For some students, stretching past four years comes only at a financial cost. For others, drifting off the four-year course has much greater costs. According to the parenting website *Grown and Flown*, some students "will take one or two extra years to complete a degree while still others may drop out, clutching a transcript of random course credits and loan statements in place of a diploma." Failing at college in this way can stunt students' academic and professional progress just as they're just beginning their adult lives. It can create significant financial and emotional obstacles.

But if so many students don't graduate in four years, your child may be wondering how to make a four-year plan a reality. Here are the key pointers to share:

- The general rule of thumb is to complete fifteen credits per semester over eight semesters. However, each university has its own formula for graduation requirements. It's critical he becomes familiar with these requirements from the get-go.

- If he wants multiple majors and/or minors, then the formula and degree requirements will change. In turn, he may need more semesters to accommodate his goals. The same may be true if he changes majors downstream. (See more details below.) As discussed in chapter 4, however, your child needs to seriously ask if the end justifies the means.

Never Too Early: A Note for High School Parents

Some of you readers may be ahead of the game and reading this book while your student is still in high school. It's never too early for parents to start planning for the freshman voyage. Likewise, it's never too early for students to start planning as well. Your child has a great opportunity to take steps today that will better his odds of graduating college in four years.

For example, you can encourage him to consider Advanced Placement classes or other college-credit opportunities offered to high schoolers. Earning college credits in high school—often for free—is a huge financial advantage. Some students begin college with a semester or more of credits under their belts. Some are even ready to launch into their degree programs because they've completed their general requirements. Just be aware, however, that these credits do not always transfer to every school. Do your homework ahead of time to learn if the credits will transfer to his university of choice.

Remember—your student is at the helm for this four-year voyage. Still, she may benefit from some mentoring to help her beat the odds and graduate "on time." For instance, even if your child has already locked into her first semester classes, she'll soon be looking at the course catalog for the second semester. Her enthusiastic brain may be thinking that Intro to Figure Skating would be a fun way to celebrate her Olympic spirit.

But if she's not a PE major and if it doesn't count toward her general education requirements, the class will probably not meet the criteria for her degree. Extra elective courses can be fun and even boost GPAs, but they can also add unnecessary credits to a transcript.

As a mentor, help her understand that if she wants a diploma in four years, any and all credits must fulfill the requirements for her general education and declared degree. (Of course, if you have unlimited funds and your student has unlimited time, the possibilities are endless! Archery 106, anyone?)

Rest assured you are not your student's only mentor in this regard. Your child will be prompted to work closely with an academic advisor to develop a timeline with the end goal of graduation in four years. One of the crew members we met in chapter 3, an academic advisor is like a skipper on a boat—a professional with the training, charts, and experience to keep your child seaworthy.

"The best thing my daughter did academically was schedule an appointment with her advisor the first week of class," says Beth, mom of a sophomore. "They discussed her goals and her dreams from day one. He's been an incredible resource for her, serving as a reference for a job off-campus and even getting her into already-full classes to keep her schedule on track."

Academic advisors understand the system and the importance of a balanced workload. Encourage your student to foster a positive relationship with her advisor and schedule an appointment anytime she has any questions throughout her college career. A quick fifteen-minute appointment with an advisor can set a student on the right course for the first year and beyond.

Changing Majors

You might as well prepare yourself now. He may tell you during a phone call. He may slip it into an e-mail. Or he may drop the bomb during a visit home. But sooner or later, it'll probably happen.

"Mom, Dad—I'm changing my major," he'll announce. "After a few classes, I realize sports medicine isn't for me. I'm changing my major to philosophy."

The changing major. Although some parents are open to such a revelation, others find it disconcerting or even frightening. Either way, this is an important time to remember your mentorship approach to parenting. It's not a time to panic or overreact.

"Among today's students, switching majors is not uncommon at all," confirms Dr. Sentwali Bakari, Drake University dean of students. For today's college students, selecting a major is not necessarily a lifelong binding contract. Students, on average, change their majors three times. Most college students—some studies suggest as many as 80 percent—change their major at least once.

After all, does anyone really expect eighteen-year-olds to know what careers they want for a lifetime? These are the same kids who, only a few short months ago, couldn't decide what to wear to prom. Understand too that doubt is a natural part of the maturing process. Many students go through a time when they question their choices (often in their second year—called the "sophomore slump").

While it may appear to parents that students change their majors as frequently as they change their relationship statuses on Facebook, the students often have valid reasons. For example, some students are tuned in to today's changing work environment. "Students see the ever-evolving career marketplace and want to capitalize on their educational investment—essentially career ROI," says Dr. Bakari.

Other students, he elaborates, may have one career in mind growing up in their home communities, only to discover a much broader spectrum of career and educational opportunities at college. Many encounter these new areas during their general courses. In this case, some students change majors, while others add a second major, minor, or area of concentration.

As explained earlier, changing and adding majors can sometimes add semesters. In some cases, the financial implications are negative. In other cases, they are quite positive. As Dr. Bakari points out, "Sometimes it only takes a few more classes to earn a double major, thereby maximizing dollars spent at the institution."

Take Joe, for example. This bright, outgoing student started his freshman year as a journalism major at a small private liberal-arts university. He took mostly general classes his first semester.

During his second semester, he was selected for an internship position with a Senate primary campaign. The experience opened his eyes to a new career path. He was hooked on politics—inspired by the historical component as well as the public relations aspects.

Today Joe is a junior with a double major in politics and strategic political communication. He's active in his fraternity and works part-time on campus. He recently returned from a semester in Austria, where he studied history, classical music, and European politics. Even with the double major, the job, the fraternity, and the study abroad experience, he expects to graduate in four years.

I can give you a firsthand example of changing majors from my own life story. You see, I went off to school with one goal in mind—to become an airline pilot. Since age three, that is all I'd ever wanted to be. When it was time for me to shop for colleges, I chose my school based on its aviation program. I declared my major—commercial aviation. I didn't have a plan B.

With my eye on a coveted captain's seat at Northwest Airlines, I registered for Intro to Aviation and took out a secondary loan to pay for flight costs. I was scheduled to fly three days a week.

I arrived early on the first day, eager to meet my flight instructor and take to the skies for my first airborne lesson. Two hours later, somewhere over the plains of North Dakota, I felt a little rumble deep within. Brushing it off as nerves, I concentrated on the panel in front of me. Altimeter. Transponder. (Rumble. Gulp.) Airspeed indicator. (Rumble.) After completing the flight and sweating through the postflight checklist, I fled to the restroom and tossed my breakfast.

This, unfortunately, became my routine on flight days. I'd fly my lesson, land, and promptly vomit. Then I'd return to my dorm room to sleep off the nausea that overtook me, missing my later classes.

I was plagued by motion sickness. Needless to say, the condition forced me to make the difficult decision to stop flying and seek a new major.

As you can see, the reasons for changing a major are as varied as the number of students who change them. Some students change because they rushed into declaring a major their hearts were never set on in the first place.

If your student seems uncertain about picking a major, reassure him there's time. Many schools recognize that the pressure to select a major can be a dilemma. Some universities offer the option of having an undeclared major for at least the first year. This provides the students the opportunity to experience a few classes and adapt to college before selecting a major.

And what should you do if you learn your student is considering a major change? Obviously, her personal reasons for changing majors will influence your parent-student conversations. Here are a few suggestions to consider if—or more likely when—you get the call:

- Don't panic. There may be very good reasons for your student to change majors. If the decision is carefully weighed, it may be the wisest choice for your student. Enable your student to take the lead in this life decision, and offer your support. Listen first, then ask questions. Positive communication is key.

- Look at both sides. As she contemplates this new major, help her reflect on why she chose her original major in the first place. Did her reasons make sense then? Did she rush? What has changed?

- Dig deeper if you sense there's more than meets the eye to this change. Is she doing poorly? Getting enough rest? Homesick? Is she facing more serious struggles, such as mental illness or addiction? (See chapter 13 for more details.)

- Discuss alternatives to changing the major. What about a double major? Adding a minor?

- Consider the financial implications. Will this add an additional semester or year? Then again, staying in the wrong major can be problematic—and expensive—too.

- Encourage your student to talk to her academic advisor, faculty members in the new department, and the career guidance office.

Grades: More Than As, Bs, and Cs

Both parents and students need to understand the academic workload is much heavier in college than in high school. Degree programs are extremely rigorous, which can be scary and frustrating for students and somewhat shocking for parents. As difficult as it may be, take a breath and relax your expectations—just a little bit. Encourage your student to apply himself and manage his time, but don't expect straight As.

"Allow your child some time to adjust to the academic culture," says Dr. Bakari. "College is a more competitive environment, and each student is different." He advises parents to be patient and recognize it will take first-year students several weeks to adapt to the environment and develop successful study and time management habits.

It's understandable that we parents want to support and motivate our children through this difficult transition. We all have different motivational techniques we've put into practice from early on in our children's lives. Some parents offer bribes of all kinds. You know the ones. They'd entice their kids to poop in the toilet with rewards of stickers, M&M's, or Matchbox cars. Did you hear about the mom who promised her daughter a doll for a potty? Imagine what that little girl demanded later in life. A shiny new bicycle for learning to tie her shoes? Diamond earrings for an A on her college report card? Where are the M&M's for college students?

Realistically, how do we motivate our college students to focus on academics over five-dollar pitchers and dart leagues? Is motivation really a parent's responsibility in the first place? I think not, and the experts agree.

At this point, we can't poke or prod or bribe or threaten. There's little we can do but be supportive mentors. We have to hope we've already instilled a work ethic and sense of responsibility in our kids. Hopefully, he'll soon learn that attendance, participation, and productivity are the essential components of student success.

As we discussed earlier, you won't see your student's report card unless he shares it with you. If he does, take a breath and keep perspective.

If you're used to him sailing through high school on the honor roll, you may be in for a little surprise when he calls home broken up over his first C. But again, parents, remember this is college and not high school. Classes are hard. This is a big transition, and transitions take time.

Be encouraging. Remind him that the true goal of college is to come out with much more than As. Advice from the experts: when students focus on learning the material rather than fixating on letter grades, the good grades usually follow.

Dealing with Academic Struggles

Maybe, though, you've noticed that your child is struggling more than expected. Is that ten-page paper causing her to lose sleep? Do you think he's in over his head in biology? Is test anxiety getting the best of her?

You may feel like swooping in, but remember this is all a part of a college student's learning curve. That being said, you do have parental instincts for a reason. A good mentor listens and knows when to be supportive and offer advice. Jessica, a college student, offers parents poignant advice: "If [students] say, 'I can't do this' or 'I want to quit,' say 'You can do it.' A lot. We need you to be strong for us when the going gets tough."

If you truly feel your student is underwater, by all means get involved. First ask if she's okay. Then ask if she's reached out to her university resources for help.

Understand that universities want their students to thrive. They realize the freshman year is a huge adjustment for many students. Universities have learning centers that provide a plethora of academic services, from drop-in tutoring to workshops on study skills, test-taking strategies, and time management. Some centers provide individual study skill assistance, while others offer courses on critical thinking and effective writing habits. They also have resources for students with ADHD and other learning concerns. Whatever services your student may need, the key is that he recognizes he needs help—and asks for it—sooner rather than later.

If your child is doing especially poorly in a particular class, he may weigh the pros and cons of withdrawing midsemester to avoid a failing grade. Bottom line for him and for you: failing grades aren't good, but one too many withdrawals can add an extra semester (or more) to Junior's collegiate career.

Keep in mind that some academic problems are self-inflicted. Perhaps your child is struggling with classes due to some poor lifestyle choices. Is she partying too much? Is he sleeping in because he thinks it's "just as good" to catch the online lecture later—even though participation and attendance are required for the grade?

It's your child's responsibility—not the university's and not even yours—to make adjustments. While colleges do provide many avenues of support, their primary goal is to provide a solid education, not to babysit your student after hours. You too can be a supportive mentor, but only your child can take action to refocus his priorities. It's part of being an adult.

That said, sometimes problems in class are signs of deeper issues elsewhere. "If it's not right in the classroom—life probably isn't good outside of it either," says Dr. Cara Halgren, University of North Dakota associate vice president and dean of students. "It's typically all connected. Very rarely do I work with students with alcohol and other drug issues (or other behavioral issues) or mental health issues that are doing really well in the classroom. And vice versa."

If you have serious concerns about your child's well-being, then you should probably contact the university. The proper protocol is generally to contact the office of student affairs or the dean of students. The folks in these departments are trained professionals with experience in handling tough student situations, such as illness, mental health problems, and more. (Again, we'll discuss such topics in chapter 13.)

Life Lessons the Hard Way

Lots of learning is accomplished between the ages of eighteen and twenty-two, both inside and outside the classroom. Ask yourself: *When did I learn my greatest life lessons? Was it during times of smooth sailing? Or was it when I nearly capsized? Were my aha moments revealed when I overcame obstacles? Did I learn from my mistakes?*

I remember sitting in Aviation 101, taking a test on the phonetic alphabet, the ABCs air traffic controllers and pilots use to communicate. I'd burned the midnight oil studying and felt well-prepared.

I worked my way through the test: Alpha, Bravo, Charlie, Delta, Echo . . . Papa, Quebec, Romeo . . . S . . . S . . . S . . . I was s-s-stuck. The S word wouldn't come to mind. I finally made something up.

When I got my test back, I had one wrong. Yes, the S. I looked up the answer. Sierra. It was Sierra. Believe me, to this day I still remember the phonetic S. I may have lost some others in the cobwebs of my brain, but I will never ever forget Sierra.

Mistakes help us learn, grow, and retain information. In fact, sometimes mistakes or bad choices create the most opportune moments for maturing. This is certainly true for first-year college students. It's important, then, to allow our children the chance to make these fruitful mistakes.

Joan, a university employee and a mother of a recent college graduate, firmly believes there's great value in giving young adults the luxury of making mistakes. "College students make mistakes, and mistakes have consequences," she explains, "and consequences provide a fertile field for learning."

This concept, while great in theory, can still be a challenge for parents. We naturally want to protect our children from negative consequences. Joan reassures parents with these wise words: "Remember—a mistake by your child does not make you a failure as a parent."

Carlie, a senior computer science major, recalls "going nuts" her freshman year and getting a little too involved in the party scene. "I went out a lot—too much, actually," she says with a shrug and an embarrassed half smile. "It caught up with me, and I missed a lot of my classes."

Her plummeting grades nearly cost her a hefty scholarship. Fortunately, the threat of lost scholarship dollars was the wake-up call she needed to realize that she did, in fact, have to show up for class to earn a degree.

Lesson learned? "Absolutely," she answers. "I'm just glad I figured it out early and was able to make up the classes and stay in school."

Her parents were glad too. Living three hours away, they were unaware of the problem at the time. When Carlie told them afterward, they realized that by handling the situation herself, she had matured more than if they had stepped in.

How do we allow our children to make mistakes and grow from them without hurting themselves or their futures? We empower them with information. How do we let go enough to let them grow? We trust them to use the foundation of knowledge and communication we've been teaching since they were born.

We must send them out to sea. Your child will learn that the captain of a boat may call on his crew, refer to his charts, or even radio back to land for assistance. Ultimately, however, he is solely responsible for making the decisions to bring his vessel safely to shore.

Focus on the Big Picture

While this is a chapter on academic expectations, it's important for parents to step back and look at the big picture. If we think about the college experience from a comprehensive perspective, we'll realize our children's education comes from so much more than textbooks and classes. Our students are not only navigating their career paths and learning the skills needed to pursue them. They're also preparing for life AC (after college).

While their frontal lobes continue to fuse, they're honing their decision-making and problem-solving skills. They're developing character and integrity and recognizing the responsibilities of adulthood. They're learning to cohabitate, communicate, and advocate. They're forging lifelong friendships and possibly meeting lifetime partners. And let's not forget they're doing all this while trying to make the dean's list!

Parents can help by recognizing that these comprehensive college experiences—in and out of the classroom—are all a part of our children's education. These experiences become tools in their tool kit for life. Graduating summa cum laude is a good thing, but graduating a confident, prepared, well-adjusted adult ready for life AC is the ultimate reward.

ELEVEN

ROOMMATE RELATIONS

The great difference between voyages rests not with the ships, but with the people you meet on them.
—AMELIA BARR

Ah, roommates. Remember the summer before college, when your child eagerly awaited word about his new roomie? Anticipating the roommate assignment was second only to anticipating the acceptance letter from First-Choice U. Your student couldn't wait to find out if he won the roommate lottery.

Remember too how he—and you—would be up all night with tornadoes of roommate scenarios swirling in your sleep-deprived brains?

- Will he show up with a bong?

- What if she's a drama queen? Or a trust fund princess?

- Does he consider cannabis germination a scientific pursuit?

- Is she a slob?

- How will he feel about your child's passion for theater?

- Will her out-of-town boyfriend be taking up residence in your daughter's room?

- What if he snores and snorts like a tugboat?

That was before the launch. For better or worse, your child is now at sea with his new shipmate. Perhaps it's been smooth sailing for them. Perhaps it hasn't. What's a parent to do, especially when the angry texts and calls come flooding in?

As you can guess, this is yet another parent-as-mentor situation. This chapter is designed to give you some talking points and insight when your student finds herself in the sometimes-choppy waters of roommate relations. (Or perhaps you're reading this prior to your child's launch. In which case, you're able to share these tips with your student even sooner—before she and her shipmate meet.)

Living with a Friend

Some students avoid the risks of the roommate lottery by living with high school friends. If this is the case with your child, you may have even tried to talk him out of it. Don't we all know friends ripped apart after rooming in college? Maybe it happened to you.

But in the naïveté of youth, students can't imagine anything ever coming between them and their BFFs. What they don't realize is that being besties is completely different than living together in a twelve-by-fourteen room seven days a week for nine months— during a time of stressful changes and adjustments.

Living with high school friends can work successfully. But many experts agree it's not always the best course of action.

Evan, a freshman, heard the warnings against living with a high school friend. He thought he and his buddy would be different. They'd been friends since childhood in their small town, playing sports and chumming around outside of school. Certain it wouldn't be an issue, they started their freshman year as roommates. By Christmas, they were no longer speaking.

"It was a bad idea from the start," he now admits. "I wish we'd have listened, because living together totally killed our friendship."

If your child is living with a friend, encourage her to mitigate the situation by extending her social circle beyond their dorm room. You can pose it this way: Does your child want to spend 24-7 only with her old friend and effectively turn her college experience an extension of high school? Or would she prefer to meet new people and grow her social circle along with her mind?

Living with a Stranger

Or perhaps your student played the roommate lottery and is living with a stranger. Many experts find this to be the preferred option. What better way to prepare for an increasingly diverse and multicultural society than to live peacefully with somebody from a completely different background?

Please understand—I'm not saying living with a stranger is always smooth sailing. It's not. But there's plenty to be gained from the experience. Living with a stranger provides ample opportunities to develop life skills. It takes a lot of guts and a little faith.

Maybe it takes a little luck too—as in, luck of the draw with how roommates are assigned. Some roommates are highly compatible. Some . . . aren't.

Before school started, Lucy had some real concerns about the roommate selection process at the university her daughter, Rose, would be attending. This anxiety started during an immersion-type overnight stay. Parents hunkered down in the comforts of the nearest Holiday Inn, and prospective students got a "real" college experience by sleeping over in the dorms with current students. Supposedly, the university brass carefully selected the host students to be school ambassadors.

Rose was introduced to Gabby, her host student and roommate for the night. She was smothered with endless chatter and a scent she couldn't quite make out on the girl. Upon arrival in the dorm room, Rose immediately began sneezing. Then she met Gabby's four-legged roommate, the source of the mystery scent. Furry and purry and definitely on the university's "do not pack" list, Peaches immediately rubbed up on Rose's pant leg, leaving a trail of fluffy white fuzz behind.

With allergies in overdrive, Rose dreaded the long stinky night next to the litter box. Fortunately, some other host students had concerns about Gabby's abilities to be an effective ambassador. They invited Rose out for the evening while Gabby and Peaches snuggled in for a night of Animal Planet.

Even after the less-than-stellar first impression (and subsequent allergy meds), Rose still chose to attend that university. Her second campus visit was another immersion experience, this one during summer orientation.

In an effort to help students meet one another, the university randomly paired incoming freshmen as roommates during orientation. The school organized ample activities and learning sessions to keep the students occupied into the wee hours of the night. Their motive? Wear the students out so they'd fall into bed exhausted and not be tempted to explore "freedom" too early.

Rose went to the residence hall to meet her randomly assigned roommate, optimistic this one would not have a cat and would be interested in more than the Animal Planet TV listings. You've heard the phrase "be careful what you wish for"? Well, Rose got what she wished for.

Her roommate, Jackie, was definitely not a feline fanatic and had no intentions of hunkering down in front of the TV. However, her idea of going out had nothing to do with the university-sanctioned group activities.

"So, where are the real parties at?" Jackie asked as she slurped from her water bottle. "Let's get outa here and have some real fun." *Sluuuurp.*

Not exactly naïve, Rose quickly discerned it was rum, not water, in the bottle. Rose politely declined the offer to go find some action. Jackie went out, and Rose connected with some other girls, spending that night on the floor of their room. Rose was not surprised when a green-around-the-gills Jackie slithered in late to the next morning's session.

Point is, roommate assignments can be a crapshoot. But I'm happy to tell you, in spite of her two initial strike-outs, Rose hit a home run with her actual roommates that fall. She was assigned to a triple (a room for three), and her roommates did not bring pets, rum, or bad attitudes.

The Instant–BFF Myth

When living with strangers, some students—usually female ones—believe they must become the best of friends. Becoming instant BFFs may seem like a fantastic idea to students. And actually, it may even provide a sense of comfort to parents. After all, there's safety in numbers. It's easy to be lulled by the thought of your student and her roomie attached at the hip 24-7.

However, being inseparable besties is usually not realistic nor is it the best-case scenario in roommate relations. Rather, the most positive roommate situations evolve out of mutual respect, kindness, and giving space. Alex, a sophomore, sums it up: "Be friendly with your roommate, but don't involve yourself too much in each other's lives. Make sure to make more friends elsewhere."

I can speak to the respectful friendship roommates can forge. Back in the dark ages, when I was preparing for college, I bravely took my chances with the roommate lottery. I left my future in the hands of someone working summer hours in the housing office.

As I recall, my roommate assignment was based on a preferences form I completed and returned to the university via mail. Snail mail. My future roommate would be determined by which box I checked:

☐ smoker
☐ nonsmoker

Yes, my relationship (or lack thereof, to be more accurate) with the Marlboro Man would dictate my fate.

Fortunately, my roommate, Dee, was a kindhearted, nonsmoking bookworm. She arrived on campus with strict orders from her parents to maintain a 4.0 grade point average or they'd pull her from college. No pressure there. Dee knew they were serious. Not wanting to head home without a degree, she spent every waking hour with her nose buried in a book.

Because of this, we never attended a party together or bonded over late-night grinders at the Red Pepper. We did, however, have a respectful relationship that grew into a warm friendship.

We respected each other's need for alone time. I learned to live quietly so she could study. She kept her things tidy after recognizing my sick need for order. I'd feed her pizza and calm her when she was up late and stressed-out before a test. She taught me 101 ways to cook beans in a hot pot and patiently tutored me in pre-algebra, a nice break from her own advanced calculus. We adjusted and adapted to each other's needs—skills that have served us both later in life.

In case you're wondering, Dee graduated with honors, attended medical school, and is now a doctor. Do you think the loving support of her first roommate had anything to do with her success?

Bunkhouse Rules and Communication

Whether your child is rooming with a high school friend or is matched up with a complete stranger, it's a huge adjustment for everybody involved. Nine months may not seem so long to us old folks, but it can feel like an eternity to nervous first-year students adapting to a new living situation. In your role as mentor, remind your student that good communication is key to roommate relations.

For those reading before the launch, encourage your child to contact her roommate as soon as the assignment letter arrives. As described in chapter 5, they can use packing as the icebreaker. Many a roommate relationship has begun with "Hey, I can bring a mini fridge. Do you happen to have a TV?"

For those with students already launched, bunked up, and far from port, there's still no time like the present. Luckily, there are strategies to help establish healthy communication before major problems arise.

A simple strategy is for the roommates to sit down and just talk—to start a dialogue about expectations and habits. For starters, listed below are a few areas of potential conflict—icebergs that can sink a ship. Again, guide your student to chat with his roomie about these issues sooner than later. The goal is to be open and honest as they set some agreed-upon rules. As in any relationship, compromise is key. By taking these preventive measures, they may able to dodge some big bumps later in the year.

Here's one example: the roomies should discuss music. While music can be a dynamite denominator over which to bond, it can also be the TNT that blows up a relationship. Sounds trite to you? Well, if your child needs peace and quiet to study and his roommate needs to blast Ozzy to "get inspired," you could be in for some frustrated phone calls. If their tastes in music or desired decibel levels are not in sync, they need to work out compromises and solutions. One such solution: noise-canceling headphones to buffer out "Crazy Train."

Another route is for them to implement a formal roommate agreement. Any fan of the *Big Bang Theory* is likely groaning right now, but Sheldon may be on to something. These written agreements do provide a foundation of communication and respect between two (or more) people. They cover many of the topics listed below but also include sections on respect, behavior, personal property, and quiet hours.

Many universities require completing a roommate agreement as a part of the residence hall check-in process. Otherwise, your child can find many samples and templates with a Google search.

Discussion Points

Whether they're simply starting an open dialogue or creating a formal roommate agreement, here are a few topics the bunkmates may want to discuss. Consider these conversation starters, not how-to advice. I'm just listing some issues here so you can share them with your student. In the end, it's up to the roomies to consider the issues, determine where they can compromise, identify the deal breakers, and create an agreement (casual or formal) that details their mutual decisions.

Sleepy time: Is the roomie nocturnal? Or does he require at least eight hours of beauty rest? How does he feel about lights on after midnight? Does she hit snooze six times before rolling out of bed? Or does she wake up with the sun?

Extracurriculars: Does she bang around the room before dawn to get to morning practice? Does the entire lacrosse team hang out on the futon? Is she rarely around because service club commitments occupy her every spare minute? Is he a music major? Does he practice his bassoon in the room? Or is his only musical talent burping the entire alphabet in the key of G?

Social life: Does she stay out until the wee hours, then stumble in to make mac and cheese for her drunk friends? Does he host all-night Minecraft marathons? Is his out-of-town girlfriend a permanent fixture on the weekends? Does she plan to host parties in the room? Does her closet look like a minibar?

Neatness: Does she consider a cup without a coaster a "mess"? Or will a *Hoarding: Buried Alive* camera crew come knocking on her door? Does he grow fuzzy green science experiments in the fridge? Does he demand that the DVDs are alphabetized?

Yours, Mine, and Ours: Is she comfortable sharing clothes— with or without asking first? Is the salsa in the fridge fair game? The beer stash? Is he okay with other people touching his gaming system? Or using her makeup?

Roommate Squabbles

Of course, even roommate agreements aren't foolproof. Problems can and do come up. According to a 2014 UCLA study, almost 50 percent of first-year students report having difficulty living together. As a mother, I do not find that statistic the least bit shocking.

Let's be honest—teenagers are not always the most considerate people. And their interpersonal communication skills often leave something to be desired. Like family members, roommates can't be expected to agree on everything all the time. Remember how she used to argue with her sister? It usually takes two to tango.

If you remember from chapter 9, parents are usually first on a student's call or text list when problems arise. I can almost guarantee that every college parent will get a call about roommate squabbles at one point.

My friend Gina got the call when her daughter returned to the dorm after work one evening to find twenty-four people partying in their suite. Yes, twenty-four. There were people on her daughter's bed, on her desk, and spilling beer on her futon. "I don't know how they did it," Gina says, remembering the call. "It's such a tiny space! They had to be packed in there like sardines." The noise triggered a visit from security, which ultimately shut down the party. Needless to say, the experience didn't help roommate relations.

So if (when) you get the angry "my roommate is evil" call from your student, start by listening. Let her vent. Your role is to be a sympathetic sounding board—a soft place to land. Then prompting her by asking a few open-ended questions such as "How have you tried to resolve it?" might enable her to develop her own solutions. If she hasn't already broached the issue with her roommate, encourage her to start a calm, honest discussion—one not in the anger of the moment. Suggest they revisit their roommate agreement.

If more than good communication is needed to resolve this issue, you can point your student in the RA's direction. The RA will be a good resource if your student needs reinforcement. These hall leaders are trained in conflict resolution and understand the challenges first-year roommates face.

If the situation is more than the RA can handle, or if proposed solutions continue to fall short, the next step is for your student—not *you*—to contact the director of residence life. This person is the RA's boss and is likely already familiar with the situation. If the situation is dangerous or unhealthy, encourage your child to meet with the director of residence life as soon as possible.

Roommate Overboard!

When all solutions fail, your child may feel the only option is to throw his roommate overboard. If your student seriously wants a new roommate, the director of residence life can help make it happen. Most schools allow this as an option if they have the space and if all other solutions have come up short. Some schools require a trial period or waiting period, especially during the first few weeks of classes, before granting the request.

According to one RA at a large Midwest university, changing roommates is possible but not always as simple as it seems. Her suggestion for a student who's completely incompatible with her roommate: if you want out, then be very flexible about your new housing assignment. In other words, students don't get to pick their new roommates or dorms. It's highly unlikely the housing office can just place a student in her "dream room." The student should also keep in mind that her next roommate will likely be someone she knows even less about than her current roommate. Maybe this roomie will be a winner. Or maybe she'll be worse than the first one.

For these reasons, the RA encourages students to seriously consider staying put and working it out. "If a student is going to be picky about where they want to live or who they'll have to live with, they might want to try to either mediate or simply learn to avoid their roommate."

Parents and students alike should keep in mind that one of the most valuable parts of the college and dorm experience is learning

TWELVE

An Ocean of Opportunities

Twenty years from now, you will be more disappointed by the things you didn't do than those you did. So throw off the bowlines. Sail away from safe harbor. Catch the wind in your sails. Explore. Dream. Discover.
—MARK TWAIN

Does this describe your situation? Your child is a few weeks into his first semester. He's finally all settled in at the dorm. He's got his schedule down pat. He has a good feel for when to hit the books and when to hit the PS4 with his roomie. (And yes, the two seem to be getting along well so far.) You're proud of how he's handled these challenging first weeks of the college experience—and proud of how you've handled them too.

But just when everything seems to be calming down, you read a certain tone in his texts, hear a hint of something in his voice. Now that the initial shock and thrill has worn off, maybe he's a little homesick. Maybe a little bored. Whatever it is, something seems just a bit off. Maybe something is missing, but he doesn't quite know what.

This is where the mentorship theory of parenting can help. Remember, good mentors listen and ask questions. Is he involved in any extracurricular activities on campus? Is he connected to a student group? Has he met students—other than his roommate—outside of classes?

Often, the key ingredient to a fulfilling college experience is extracurricular activities. Experienced parents and college administrators both consistently convey this message: *encourage your child to get involved in campus activities.*

Clubs and organizations provide creative, mental, and sometimes physical outlets for students to broaden their perspectives and simply burn off some steam. Being involved can help prevent homesickness by keeping students' minds occupied with something other than missing Mom or Dad. Most importantly, these groups provide a new circle of friends—a vital component of a positive college experience. Even college students themselves agree. As Jessica, a senior, states, "Encourage your son or daughter to get involved at school. The people they meet their first year will become their support system throughout college."

And don't forget that this is perhaps the right time for *you* to get involved too. No, I'm not suggesting you show up at your child's next art club meeting with paintbrush in hand. But there are ways for parents to get involved, stay connected, and show their support.

We'll discuss that later. But first, let's get you prepared with some helpful advice for the next time you hear that hint of something *off* in his voice.

Helping Your Student Get Involved

College campuses have something for everyone. For every interest, there's a club or group. Most activities are inexpensive and available on or near campus. Where else can you try fencing, attend a CIA lecture, and volunteer at a nursing home dance all on the same weekend?

Many schools organize an all-campus activity fair, usually sometime in the first weeks of school. Typically, the campus ballroom or some other large gathering space is filled with tables of students promoting their groups and organizations. There's a carnival atmosphere with participants eager to entice new members. The campus activity fair is a great place for first-year students to learn about the organizations and activities available to them. As an added bonus, current college students say it's also a great place to get lots of free stuff.

Ever thought about ways your student could get involved? Want to help steer her in the right direction? Think about your child's interests, hobbies, skills, and career ambitions. Here are just a few examples of ways she can be active on campus:

Athletics/Physical Fitness: Even if your student isn't playing on a collegiate athletic team, she can still participate in intramural leagues or take fitness classes. Just about every recreational sport you can think of is available: volleyball, basketball, rowing, tennis, Quidditch (yes, seriously), Cross-Fit training, badminton, rock climbing, skiing, and scuba, to name a few. Many schools also have on-campus fitness centers available to students. If your student wants to work up a sweat, there are endless opportunities.

Foreign Languages/Cultures: It's easy—your student picks a language (French, Mandarin, Spanish, Russian, etc.) and joins a club. Is he interested in learning more about life in India? The culture of Kenya? The food in Vietnam? Encourage him to call the international student center to learn more. If interested, you, as parents, can broaden your own cultural experience by signing up to host international students during holidays and breaks.

Drama/Theater/Speech: Drama club isn't just for thespians. Along with acting, it involves lighting, music, set and costume design, and marketing. Movie clubs watch and discuss films, from the classics to newly released independents. Speech teams, debate teams, and mock trial teams travel to compete against students at other universities.

Arts and Crafts: Is glitter her favorite color? She'll find craft clubs of all kinds—knitting, scrapbooking, painting, and more. Just don't be surprised if she requests Mod Podge in her next care package. If fine arts are more her thing, she's in the right place too. College campuses are generally rich in music and fine arts programming. From ballet and choral concerts to jazz and art galleries, she will satisfy her artistic cravings.

Faith Groups: Concerned about your student not finding a church-home on campus? From organized religion to faith-based volunteerism, your child will have countless opportunities to explore or nurture his faith. Rest assured, there are faith groups eager to provide support and welcome him into a faith community.

Politics: Your child can test the political waters with the Young Republicans or College Democrats or choose to get involved in student government. Who knows? Your baby could be the next student body president.

Social Justice: In these clubs and organizations, students learn to advocate for causes they believe in, such as gender equality, LGBTQ rights, environmental protection, and global issues. Your child may come home for the holidays crusading for causes you've never even thought about.

Volunteering: Volunteerism is alive and well with college students today. Community organizations appreciate the energy and support they receive from college students. Your child can lend a hand in a variety of places, such as a soup kitchen, a nursing home, an after-school children's program, or the Humane Society.

Campus Activities: From planning dorm events to working for campus radio to being tour guides and student ambassadors, there's no shortage of opportunities for your child to develop a new skill set right on campus. Most areas of study offer extracurricular activities as well. For example, there are robot-building competitions for the engineering students and the campus newspaper for journalism majors.

Please know this is merely a sampling of opportunities in which your student can choose to get involved. Encourage her to try something new—just for fun. Now's the time for her to broaden her horizons. It may just be the missing piece to give her a new, exciting outlook and help make the most of her college experience. Just don't be surprised when she calls home telling you she needs a horse because she wants to join the water polo team. (Don't worry—she'll figure it out after the first meeting.)

It's All Greek to Me!

Another way your child can get involved on campus is to explore the Greek system, if one is in place on the university.

I know, I know—*the Greek system?* I took an informal poll and asked people what came to mind when they heard the words *fraternity* and *sorority.* Here are some typical responses:

"*Animal House.*"

"Dirty oversized houses with sticky floors from overflowing kegs."

"Entitled rich boys drinking their way through college."

"Sex, drugs, and toga parties."

"Secret meetings where they drink goat's blood and beat each other with paddles."

"Excessive alcohol."

"*Legally Blonde.*"

These folks, like many people, had no personal Greek experiences to pull from. So they were quick to draw opinions from less-than-flattering movie portrayals of Greek life. Thanks to Hollywood, negative stereotypes of the Greek system are alive and well.

Now, I'm not saying Hollywood has it all wrong. Bad things do sometimes happen in fraternities and sororities. I've watched the news footage of students trashing hotels, breaking laws, and even dying from alcohol poisoning. I've heard stories of hazing and misconduct. That being said, it's important to understand these incidents and behaviors are not the norm. In fact, these actions are not tolerated by most Greek chapters.

The Red Solo Cup—Not Just for Greeks

Let's be honest: drinking on campus is not unique to the Greek system. Sororities and fraternities do not have the corner market on alcohol consumption any more than any other group of students. Alcohol is just as prevalent at a non-Greek house party as it is a fraternity house party.

Many college students are away from home for the first time and at an age when socializing involves alcohol. Whether a student participates in drinking is a personal choice only she can make. This is true in the dorms, at off-campus parties, at bars, and at fraternities and sororities. (We'll cover alcohol use in greater detail in chapter 13.)

There's much more to the Greek system than Hollywood leads people to believe. Each sorority and fraternity has its own personality, reputation, philanthropy, and values. Even if you polled a dozen people who do have firsthand Greek experiences, you'd get a dozen different answers.

For example, my husband fondly remembers his fraternity as a place for, yes, organized beer drinking. I, on the other hand, recall the bonds of sisterhood and formal dinners at my sorority. I remember organizing events together, raising philanthropy dollars, and sharing clothes with my fifty-five housemates. You read that correctly—fifty-five women under one roof. Looking back on my college experience, I am grateful for the lifelong friendships and the extended alumnae network I've gained through my sorority.

Despite what is portrayed on the silver screen, many Greek organizations take their members' academic rankings very seriously. Most have minimum GPA requirements members must meet in order to participate in social events. Others invite favorite professors to special dinners and host academic achievement banquets.

So if your student expresses interest in learning more about Greek organizations, start by encouraging her to check out recruitment week (formerly known as rush). This is a week of organized activities that allow prospective and current Greek members to get to know one another. Universities often employ a director of Greek life with an advisory board to oversee recruitment and ensure appropriate rules are followed throughout the year.

And if your child tells you she wants to join a Greek organization, here's how to talk about it with a healthy perspective and an open mind:

- **$$$:** Some fraternities and sororities are more expensive than others. Ask to see a statement that includes fees, dues, and other expenses (events, social activities, fundraisers, etc.) for which your child will be responsible.

- **Philanthropy:** Does the house have a spirit of philanthropy? If so, what is it and how do they support it?

- **Academic expectations:** What is the GPA ranking of the sorority or fraternity? Do they require a minimum GPA to participate in social activities?

- **Social events:** Are they mandatory or optional? Do they add extra expense? How is alcohol use handled?

- **Room and board:** Will your child be expected to live in the house? What are the sleeping arrangements? Meal plan? Resident responsibilities?

- **Why?:** What are your student's reasons for joining? Is it the camaraderie? The living situation? The social opportunities? Or to broaden his college experience?

Fundamentally, the Greek system is about friendships. Brotherhood and sisterhood. Members are also given opportunities to interact with and lead their peers—a vital skill set for post-college life.

Nikki Heyd—principal subcontracts program manager at Rockwell Collins and an advisor for two Kappa Alpha Theta chapters—explains how Greek membership teaches skills key to getting and keeping jobs. "If a young woman can handle the logistics and demands of being the new-member educator for a pledge class of thirty-five, then she's developed the skill set to manage projects and communicate with a group of colleagues."

Parental Involvement

There are ample opportunities for not only students to get involved—parents can be engaged as well. But again, this is college, not high school. Parental involvement looks a little different than what you may be used to. Universities work hard to communicate with and involve parents while still maintaining the integrity of the students' private information. That is, you can be aware of what's happening on campus without cramping your child's style or being overly involved.

If you're a parent who likes to be in the know, start by visiting the school website. Most schools have a parent portal for detailed information geared specifically toward you—maps and events, tuition payment information, academic calendar, parent handbook, student services, and campus information. While you're there, check out the campus calendar. You'll learn more about the academic schedule, such as when midterms and finals week fall. You'll also find out about campus events and opportunities, which will help you understand why he's too busy to call every day.

If you're on Facebook or Twitter, see if your child's university has parent groups. It can be a great way to connect with other parents on a more personal level. These sites come in handy for bouncing ideas off other parents and seeking advice from folks on the same emotional voyage as you. Some universities have parent organizations where you can meet face-to-face at events throughout the year.

A special way to get involved and show your support is to attend parent-and-family weekend. It's a nice opportunity for you to check in once your student has had a little time to adjust to college life. For some families, it's the first visit since the highly charged move-in day. Most parents are reassured to discover that their children (and they themselves) are in much calmer emotional waters now.

Before you head to campus for parent-and-family weekend, check to see what your student needs from home. It may be a practical time to switch from summer to winter clothing, as described in chapter 5. Or he may want you to bring his soccer cleats, as he recently joined an intramural team.

Parent-and-family weekend is often packed with activities such as concerts, ice cream socials, sporting events, service projects, and faculty receptions. Some schools even offer parents the opportunity to sit in on classes. While you surely don't need to attend all the events, I suggest picking a couple with your student and checking them out. You'll get a taste of student life and make connections with other parents.

Students are usually pretty excited to introduce their new friends and show parents around campus, including their now-lived-in dorm room. Just don't let the made bed fool you. Her room may look great on the surface, but you have no idea what lies beneath and within. Whatever you do, never ever open the wardrobe. The last thing you want is to unleash the two-month supply of sweaty socks, freebie T-shirts, and dirty underwear she packed into it moments before you arrived. Trust me on this.

If you want to surprise your student with something unexpected on parent-and-family weekend, bring a stash of inspirational notes to hide around her room—a little something she can find after you leave. Check out chapter 9 and the appendix for ideas. Slip a note under a pillow, one in a shoe, and another in the fridge. It probably goes without saying, but don't try to hide one in the wardrobe. You've already been warned.

Parent-and-family weekend offers many ways to engage in your student's new experience. It's a little like hopping on his ship for a weekend excursion. It can be a simple visit or a jam-packed event. Be aware, however, that your student may be more focused on eating dinner off campus and hitting Target on your credit card than in participating in too many group events.

To make the most of the weekend, remember that he's the captain and you're the guest. Let him take the lead. That's what good mentorship is all about.

THIRTEEN

Tsunami!

The fishermen know that the sea is dangerous and the storm terrible, but they have never found these dangers sufficient reason for remaining ashore.
—Vincent van Gogh

College is a time for growing into adulthood. That often means experimenting: sex, alcohol, drugs, to name a few. We had eighteen-plus years to (hopefully) instill our values in our children. Now is the time for them to figure out how to evaluate and apply those values to their own circumstances. This is when young adults establish their own value systems, develop life skills, and learn—via both successes and mistakes—that actions have consequences.

Prior to our daughter leaving for college, I asked for advice from Shelly, an experienced mom of two college students. Her advice was direct: "Don't be naïve, but don't meddle."

Her let-them-figure-it-out approach is the same advice you'd hear from numerous college administrators and staff. These professionals are sympathetic to the plight of first-time college parents, but they also want to support the personal growth and development of students. (Remember the discussion in chapter 10 about mistakes being the best life lessons?)

I know I shouldn't meddle. But as a parent of a college student, I have fears—huge, irrational fears—about the darker side of the college experience: rape, alcohol poisoning, drug overdoses. Not to mention crime, depression, eating disorders, and more. I fear the things I cannot control.

I cringe at news stories of college students making bad choices and hurting themselves or others. Those stories aren't fiction. They're real. They're people. They're somebody's kids.

Unfortunately, I can't write an honest book about parenting college students without addressing these heavy topics. Most of us would rather pretend they didn't exist. But they do. This is the real, sometimes scary stuff we can't ignore.

That said, please know this chapter is not designed to scare the wind out of your sails. Some topics here are not "bad" things when handled in a mature way. But as parents, we cannot assume maturity will always prevail with our college-aged children. Some mistakes are life lessons. Other mistakes are life threatening. As mentors, it's still our job to support them and guide them in the basics of safety, protection, and self-care.

I urge you to have multiple conversations with your student about this heavy stuff. If you're reading this before you send your student-captain out to sea, set the packing list aside and make time for this discussion. If your student has already shipped out, start a conversation the next time he checks in. Much of the information in this chapter is advice you can pass on to your student. (And some of it is advice you can take to your own heart.)

My hope is that this chapter will give you a starting point for discussion and resources to call upon if your child tumbles into some rough water.

Crime and Safety

Crime is no stranger to a college campus. A campus is a community, and it faces the challenges of any other community. Fortunately, most colleges focus on crime prevention from the get-go.

Like other campus safety departments, the department of public safety at Princeton University plays a role in providing a safe and secure environment 24 hours a day, 365 days a year. They believe the best protection against campus crime is an aware and informed community along with a strong public safety presence.

At Princeton, students are encouraged to utilize the services, initiatives, and trainings the department offers on a daily basis. These range from safety presentations to self-defense courses. The Princeton department of public safety maintains close partnerships with the federal, state, and local law enforcement agencies to further benefit the security of the Princeton community. Other universities form the same type of partnerships as well.

When it comes to safety on any campus (and anywhere, really), nothing is more important than common sense. Prevention is key. Scott Law, Drake University director for campus public safety, explains that most crimes are the result of motive and convenience. He encourages students to control what they can and limit the window of opportunity for the criminals. When it comes to personal safety, here are some tips to pass along to your student:

> **Be aware of surroundings.** After some time on campus, students are often lulled into a false sense of security due to their comfort level and familiarity. It's important, however, that your student always remain alert and aware. For instance, ask your student to skip the earbuds when walking

so she can pay attention to what's happening around her. She should always walk in well-lit, well-traveled areas.

Never walk alone at night. While many college campuses are self-contained—a community within a community—and have security systems in place, bad stuff can still happen. Especially at night. It may not seem like such a big deal to walk home alone from the library after it closes, but it is a bad idea. Encourage your child to venture out after dark only in pairs or groups.

Trust instincts. Tell your student to trust his instincts whenever something doesn't "feel" or "look" right. Urge him to leave the area and call for assistance.

Use safety resources. Call boxes, safety officers, and escort programs are available for a reason. Many universities offer public safety apps that students can load onto their phones for an extra layer of protection.

Theft on campus often occurs as a crime of opportunity as well. From unlocked dorm rooms to unwatched computers or backpacks, plenty of opportunities exist.

"I'm always amazed at how shocked kids are when they leave a thousand-dollar laptop unattended on a library table while they make a coffee run and return to find it missing," said one campus security officer. "Students are often trusting and don't use common sense in a situation like this, where the crime was clearly preventable."

Here are some simple pointers your student should know for theft prevention:

Use common sense and caution. Don't leave valuables in plain view in an automobile. Be cautious if a stranger asks to use your cell phone. Don't be afraid to say no.

Lock doors. An unattended, unlocked dorm room is an open invitation for theft. Scott Law's advice? "Lock your door even if you're just running down the hallway for five minutes, because five minutes is never just five minutes on a college campus."

Report theft ASAP. If something is stolen, report it to authorities immediately. Contact credit card companies to freeze accounts if your wallet is stolen. (See chapter 4 about keeping credit card phone numbers with your financial files.)

Alcohol

While underage drinking is illegal, it still happens. Why do college students choose to drink? The answers are as varied as the students themselves: to fit in, to socialize, to celebrate, to relieve stress, to bend to peer pressure.

No campus is immune. Even religious-based, covenant-signing colleges have students who drink. In fact, experts list alcohol as the number-one problem on campuses across the nation. Universities report that alcohol usage leads to poor grades, wasted time, wasted money, vandalism, fights, illness, and sexual assaults. Alcohol has become such a big issue that many colleges are establishing policies to become dry campuses.

Regardless of policies, though, your child will likely encounter booze during his college years. Should this scare you as a parent? Yes. The worst-case scenarios involving alcohol (alcohol poisoning, drowning, arrests, sexual assault, car accidents) aren't make-believe. These are real consequences for poor choices. In particular, binge drinking is a huge problem—and not a new one.

But don't be paralyzed by your fears. As parents and mentors, we can educate our kids about alcohol and share our values, then leave the rest up to them. They will have choices to make, but at least you can help prepare them for that decision-making process.

Experts agree that, ideally, parents should start talking about alcohol long before their children enter high school. If you haven't talked much about drinking over the years, it's never too late. Now's the time. Share your values and beliefs as well as your own experiences, both positive and negative.

Yes, share even the bad stuff. It's okay to tell her how scared you were when your college roommate ended up in the ER getting her stomach pumped after a party. Explain how partying like a rock star might look cool, but scraping crusted vomit from the back seat of a car the next day isn't so glamorous. Discuss the reality of "beer goggles" impairing morals. More importantly, talk about the life-altering consequences of date rape and drunk driving—for all people involved.

Here are some conversation guides, whether this is your first talk about alcohol or your hundredth.

College Isn't High School

Maybe your child never had so much as a drop of alcohol in high school. Or maybe she experimented a little at a couple of parties.

Or maybe your child arrived on campus with substance abuse problems or heavy-drinking habits carried over from high school. If your child falls into this latter category, don't be shocked if her behavior continues or even increases in college. It won't magically stop once the acceptance letter arrives.

No matter what lifestyle your child led in high school when it came to drinking, discuss with her how the college scene can be different and more intense. Students drink the most during their first six weeks of freshman year, according to the National

Institute on Alcohol Abuse and Alcoholism (NIAAA). Taylor, a junior, explains, "If freshmen drank in high school, it was like a big secret to keep it hidden. When they get to college, where everyone is encouraging them to drink openly, they just go nuts."

It's Okay to Say No

While many students do drink, many do not. Empower your child to honor his own values and be responsible. If he chooses not to drink, assure him that's okay. Drinking and peer pressure all boil down to one important question: Who decides if and what you drink? Help your student understand that *he* gets to decide.

Remind him that any reason for not drinking is a valid reason. For the times he may be faced with peer pressure, have him practice ways to say no.

- "No thanks. I'm not drinking tonight."

- "No thanks. I'm the designated driver."

- "No thanks. I need a clear head for a big test tomorrow."

- "No thanks. I prefer soda."

- Or simply, "No thanks."

Consequences Are Real

When our kids were babies, they quickly learned what "hot" meant, usually from a bad experience. All it took was one burn to understand and remember the consequence of touching a hot curling iron. Painful lesson? Yes. Effective? Absolutely.

There are many potential consequences of underage or binge drinking for college students. Unfortunately, these consequences often take more than a Band-Aid and some burn gel to heal. They can leave lasting scars on lives and alter futures. Lay out some all-too-real scenarios for her:

- Hangovers + inability to focus + missing class = bad grades and perhaps lost scholarship or potentially dropping out

- Too many drinks + compromised judgment + lack of safety = sexual assault

- Binge drinking + falling asleep + vomit = death by asphyxiation

- Drinking games + binge drinking = alcohol poisoning and perhaps death

Each one of these scenarios becomes a possibility when drinking is out of control. The NIAAA reports that 1,825 college students between the ages of eighteen and twenty-four die each year from alcohol-related injuries. Good kids make bad choices with traumatic results. Talk with your child about the *real* consequences that can come with having a "good time."

Parents Have Expectations

I'm not here to tell you what to believe. We all have different ideas about alcohol based on our own experiences, morals, health, and education. And we all have different expectations about our students drinking.

Some folks feel it's okay, even healthy, to share a few drinks with their underage students so they'll have a safe opportunity to learn its effects. Some parents are teetotalers and expect their children to abstain as well. Those with a family history of alcoholism may choose to not partake and may share their knowledge with their children. Still others take the "kids will be kids" approach and look the other way even if they know their children are drinking.

No matter what your personal or moral stance may be, please take the initiative to at least talk with your student about your expectations regarding alcohol. While there's no guarantee she'll honor your expectations to a T, she'll know where you're coming from when you say, "You'll probably go to a few parties, but you need to clearly understand that your schoolwork must come first. If booze gets in the way of academics, we won't continue to pay for your tuition." Remember—you are a mentor, and this choice is in her hands. But it's good to let her know you're aware and that you care.

Set Personal Limits and Rules

If your child plans to drink (and again, let's face it—many kids have experience with this in high school), urge him to consider setting personal limits or hard lines he will not cross. Personal limits can work as preventive tools for some (often lethal) consequences of binge drinking.

When talking to a group of current college students who admitted to drinking, I asked if they had personal limits or rules of engagement. Use their responses as a jumping-off point to introduce the concept of personal limits with your student.

- "We always have a designated driver."

- "No shots—ever."

- "I just say 'I don't like beer,' and it lets me off the hook because all the parties I go to only serve keg beer."

- "Friends don't let drunk friends hook up."

- "We have a buddy system with the girls on our floor. We only go out as a group and always look out for each other."

- "I usually go BYOB so I know exactly what I'm drinking."

- "I limit myself to two drinks and then switch to soda."

Drink Safe and Smart

In an environment where drinking can lead to alcohol poisoning, date rape, and impaired driving, here are some suggestions from current college students about playing it safe and smart:

- **Don't accept a drink from someone else.** If it comes in a keg, pour it yourself. If it comes in a bottle or can, open it yourself. If it's in a red Solo cup, mix it yourself. Whatever you drink, get it yourself, then guard it with your life so nobody adds anything to it. And by all means, don't drink the punch.

- **Don't binge drink.** Don't do shots or play drinking games. Pace yourself. Set a limit before you start drinking, and keep track of what you consume. Eat before you drink to slow the absorption of alcohol. Space your drinks—alternate soda or water between drinks.

- **Never ever drink and drive.** Impaired driving kills—it's as simple as that. So don't *ever* get behind the wheel if you've been drinking. All it takes is one drink to be "driving under the influence." A cab fare is way cheaper than a DUI or the lifetime cost of ending a life.

Know When to Call 911

Alexis was spending Saturday night alone in her dorm suite, trying to get ahead on a project, when she received an alarming text. One of her roommates was passed out drunk and lying naked on the floor of a campus building.

Alexis and another roommate went out and found their friend unresponsive. Terrified, they debated calling 911. Other students quickly talked them out of it, saying, "She does this all the time," and "She'll be okay." They explained that two weeks earlier, she'd had a similar episode with drinking too much and returning to the room naked. "She was fine then," they said. "She'll be fine now. It's just what she does."

Back in the suite, Alexis spent the next six hours monitoring her friend's breathing and ensuring she didn't choke on her vomit. Ultimately, the girl did wake up and laughed it off as no big deal.

"It is a big deal, a very big deal," exclaims Alexis's mom. Her frightened, sleep-deprived daughter called the next day to tell her about the experience, saying, "Mommy, I was just so scared. She wouldn't wake up."

"We really were unprepared for the enormity of drinking on a huge public university," says her mom. "I really thought I prepared my daughter for everything, even arming her with pepper spray for those nighttime classes. But never did I dream that I would have to school her on *other* people's drinking. It just never crossed my mind."

Alexis now knows if there's a next time, she will call 911 or campus security for help, no matter what other students say.

This situation is a wake-up call for parents. We need to tell our kids about alcohol poisoning for their sake's and their friends'. They need to know that simply placing a passed-out friend on his side and watching to make sure he doesn't vomit is not enough.

Tell your child to never assume someone will "sleep off" alcohol poisoning. Even when the individual is unconscious or has otherwise stopped drinking, alcohol continues to release into his bloodstream and the level of alcohol in his body continues to rise. Make your student aware of these signs and symptoms of alcohol overdose, which require seeking medical help immediately.

Signs and Symptoms of Alcohol Overdose

- Mental confusion

- Coma, inability to wake up

- Vomiting

- Seizures

- Irregular breathing

- Low body temperature, pale or bluish skin color

When a friend shows signs of alcohol overdose, let your student know it's more important to do the right thing—even if he's uncomfortable—and call 911 for help if he suspects a friend may be in trouble. It could save a life. In many states, your child and the friend will both be offered medical amnesty (see below).

What Is Medical Amnesty?

Because underage drinking is illegal, some young adults avoid calling for help when a friend shows signs of alcohol overdose. They're afraid of the legal consequences for their friend and themselves. To address this, many states offer medical amnesty, a law designed to ensure people receive prompt medical attention when at risk for alcohol overdose.

With medical amnesty, if a person under age twenty-one calls 911 for emergency assistance (for himself or a friend), both he and the friend are immune from criminal penalties related to underage drinking or possession of alcohol. In order to be exempt from punishment under this law, the person calling must remain with the person needing assistance until help arrives.

Following a medical amnesty incident, the student(s) does not receive the harsher penalty for underage drinking or drug use. Rather, he usually receives some sort of professional counseling to help identify if he has a serious alcohol or drug problem and to provide suggestions on how to stay safe in the future. A 2006 study conducted at Cornell University revealed that one such medical amnesty policy, along with a significant media campaign, dramatically increased the number of alcohol-related calls for emergency assistance.

Know How to Get Help and Support

Are you concerned your child may have a drinking problem? Where can she go for help? Where can you go for support?

Universities offer many layers of alcohol education and support for students. They may host residence hall programs, peer support groups, on-campus recovery groups, and campus awareness initiatives. The student health center can provide direction and referrals to counseling services or treatment programs. Some colleges offer substance-free dorms or recovery-based sober housing options.

You can find more specific information on your student's college website. You can also find more information and support from these organizations:

- **www.al-anon.org:** Al-Anon and Alateen offer hope and help to families and friends of alcoholics.

- **www.aa.org:** Alcoholics Anonymous (AA) is a fellowship of men and women who share their experience, strength, and hope that they may solve their common problem and help others recover from alcoholism.

- **www.sadd.org:** The mission of Students Against Destructive Decisions (SADD) is to provide students with the best prevention and intervention tools possible to deal with the issues of underage drinking, drug use, impaired driving, and other destructive decisions.

- **AwareAwakeAlive.org:** This nonprofit organization equips youth and communities with the tools and confidence to create a world in which no young life is cut short due to alcohol poisoning.

- **CollegeDrinkingPrevention.gov:** Created by the National Institute on Alcohol Abuse and Alcoholism, this site is a resource for comprehensive research-based information on issues related to alcohol abuse and binge drinking among college students.

Prescription and OTC Drugs

When you think about college and drugs, do you imagine kids smoking marijuana in their dorm room with a dryer sheet over a toilet paper roll? Think again. While recreational drugs such as marijuana, cocaine, heroin, and Ecstasy are still problems, drugs on campus take on a new look these days.

Monica received a distressing middle-of-the-night phone call. Her daughter, Marie, was in the ER. Marie attended a prestigious out-of-state university, where she was active on campus and involved in student government. She worked hard on her schoolwork and earned good grades. She had a large group of friends and adapted quickly to college life. She'd never given her parents reason to worry.

Imagine their surprise when they received the awful call

194

telling them Marie had been admitted to the hospital for a prescription drug overdose. "We were shocked and terrified," Monica explains.

After the ER experience, Marie told her parents what had happened. She and some friends obtained prescription Adderall to help them stay awake and study for finals. (More on Adderall below.) That night, after Marie's last test, this group of friends went to an off-campus hotel to celebrate the end of the semester. They drank and took some more of the "happy pills"—to dangerous results.

Security found Marie "out of it," wandering alone around the property. She wound up in the ER getting her stomach pumped. Fortunately, she had no lasting health consequences. She did, however, get the scare of her life. "She was so lucky that it was security who found her, and not someone dangerous," her mom said through tears.

Unfortunately, this is not an uncommon story. Substance abuse among young adults is not limited to alcohol or even recreational drugs. Behavior experts believe the number of prescription and over-the-counter drug overdoses is growing at an alarming rate for today's college-age students. Among adults ages eighteen to twenty-five, abuse of prescription drugs is second only to abuse of marijuana, according to the 2010 National Survey on Drug Use and Health.

Obtaining stimulants from friends with legitimate prescriptions seems less dangerous and illegal than buying recreational drugs off the street. As one student says, "It's not something that I worry about too much, because everybody's doing it." Unfortunately, this line of thinking can be catastrophic.

Please take time to talk with your child about the realities of drug use, specifically prescription or over-the-counter abuse. It's real. It happens. Kids who've never given their parents a reason to worry are getting caught up in it during their college years.

While students abuse many different drugs, here are three commonly found on college campuses today:

Adderall

Adderall (amphetamine and dextroamphetamine) is known as "the study drug" on college campuses. It was developed to treat attention deficit hyperactivity disorder (ADHD). It is widely abused, however, by students without an ADHD diagnosis. In fact, according to the National Institute on Drug Abuse, one in five college students admits to using Adderall without an ADHD diagnosis.

Students often obtain the drug from friends who have been diagnosed with ADHD and have a valid prescription. Students without ADHD report a heightened sense of motivation and focus when using Adderall, which can seemingly help when pulling an all-nighter before finals. They believe it will help them perform better academically.

What students don't seem to grasp is that Adderall, when taken without having ADHD, is highly addictive and full of side effects. Short-term side effects include sleep difficulties, irritability, nervousness, headaches, loss of appetite, change in sex drive, and depression. The long-term risk of psychological and physical dependence is a concern for routine users who feel they can't function optimally without it.

OTC Cold Medicine

Over-the-counter drugs, including cold medicines, are a growing drug problem among college and high school students. The OTC drugs of choice among today's young adults are cough and cold medicines containing dextromethorphan (DXM), a common cough suppressant. Students choose cold medications to get high because they don't need access to a prescription to obtain the medicine. They see it as inexpensive and easy.

A student who wants to get high from cough or cold medicine will typically drink an entire eight-ounce bottle or take a full package of the medicine in pill form. The medication generates hallucinations and dissociative, out-of-body experiences. OTC drugs can also act as a gateway to other drug use. Like prescription drugs, OTC cold medicines can be dangerous and addictive if abused.

OxyContin

OxyContin is a narcotic pain reliever. OxyContin is an opioid, like heroin. It is easily attainable and cheap—appealing to college students, who are increasingly taking the drug and becoming addicted. Each year the number of students overdosing on the drug rises.

Often, those who begin using OxyContin develop tolerances quickly and therefore abuse larger amounts of the drug in a short amount of time. The drug can damage the brain and impair judgment. Misuse of OxyContin increases the risk of personal injury and accidents and can lead to risky sexual behavior, misuse of other drugs, and even death.

S–E–X

For many of us, this is *the* dreaded topic. Who really wants to think about their child's sex life? Honestly, I don't want to think about my kids having sex any more than they want to think about me doing the wild thing.

Rest assured, I'm not here to condone students' sexual activity. But I am here to address it. Unfortunately, sex is another area in which parents tend to make assumptions so they can avoid talking about it with their kids. But instead of pretending sex doesn't happen on campus, be bold, be brave, and broach the subject with as much openness as you can muster.

Today's sexual culture is more open than our generation's. Conversation is commonplace. On college campuses, hookups don't refer to cable TV. Coming Out Week is widely celebrated. Contraception is readily available. Students talk about sex. Frankly, like it or not, many students are having sex.

When talking about sex with their students, many parents take the obvious, simple route: "Don't do it. End of discussion." While good in theory, this approach isn't particularly effective. Abstinence may be ideal in some parents' minds, but it is not entirely realistic in some students' lives. Interestingly, more than $1.5 billion has been spent on abstinence-only-until-marriage education since the 1990s. Despite these efforts, statistics show there has been little to no change in college students' sexual behaviors.

After all, sex is as complex as the people involved. In a collegiate environment, it can become even more complicated. College freshmen are plunked into close quarters with a variety of people with different values and ideas about sex. The combination of emerging self-discovery, still-developing mental maturity, raging hormones, and newfound freedoms creates a hotbed (pun intended) of sexual temptation.

Once again, a good place to begin as a mentor-parent is to have a healthy, honest conversation. If you're nervous, just say so. Believe me—your child will likely be uncomfortable too. You could always break the ice by commenting on a scene from a recently watched TV show, commercial, or movie. It won't be difficult to find one with a sexual undertone. Ask what he thinks about it. Then just listen. Listen as closely to him as you'd like him to listen to you.

As the conversation continues, be honest and factual. But understand you don't have to be a sexual health expert to share your values and discuss abstinence, contraception, STIs, or relationships. (More on these topics below.)

Remember this is a conversation, not a lecture. And be prepared—you may learn more from your child than you teach. Again, this generation has an openness that may surprise you. Keep in mind sex is just one of many issues he is addressing in his life. Empower your child to have the ability and the responsibility to make the key decisions himself.

LGBTQ

As college students explore their sexuality and identity, LGBTQ questions may arise. This acronym represents people who identify as lesbian, gay, bisexual, transgender, and queer and/or questioning.

Some students head off to college unsure about who they are and where they belong. There's a lot of pressure in most high schools to fit in and conform. This means that a lot of LGBTQ teenagers have to "play straight" for years.

In college, however, these restrictions often disappear. Universities can be wonderful places of acceptance and self-exploration. There are many openly LGBTQ students and faculty on campus, which creates an instant community for students coming out.

If your child identifies as LGBTQ and comes out to you, you may feel a variety of conflicting emotions, including compassion, guilt, anger, relief, confusion, shock, and denial. Whatever your reaction, please remember it took courage for your child to share this information. While it can be a lot to take in, remember your child needs your love and support now more than ever.

You may find it helpful to talk with somebody who has been through this process. Join a family support group, such as pflag. org, for a place to ask questions, receive support, and obtain educational materials to help both you and your child. Encourage your student to locate a support group on campus where people are recognized and respected for their individuality, inclusive of their sexuality. Most schools will have resources, support, counselors, and organizations for students and friends of students who identify as LGBTQ.

Birth Control

Choosing a reliable birth control method is an important part of being a sexually mature adult. Believe me—I know it's difficult to think of your baby as a "sexually mature adult." But I promised you real talk about real stuff we can't ignore, and birth control is one of those things.

The good news is, 85 percent of today's college students use at least one form of birth control every time they have sex, according to a twenty-year study by Dr. Sandy Caron, author of *The Sex Lives of College Students: A Quarter Century of Attitudes and Behaviors.* That's up from 75 percent in the 1990s. If students are choosing to have sex, at least they understand the importance of safe sex.

Sexually active students have many options when it comes to contraception: shots, pills, rings, patches, emergency contraception, and various barrier methods (such as sponges, diaphragms, and cervical caps). The two most popular methods are condoms and the pill.

Pills are about 90 percent effective at preventing pregnancy. In case you're not a math major, that is *not* 100 percent. My theory on birth control is that there's no reason not to use two forms of contraception each time. For example, the pill and a condom. Double the protection, double the safety. Doubling up also shares the responsibility—and accountability—between partners. It takes two to tango, so it should also take two to be proactive about safe sex.

Note there's no MD behind my name, so please don't swap my thoughts on birth control for the advice of a gynecologist. Instead, if you have a daughter, encourage her to talk to her doctor (or schedule a confidential appointment with student health services on campus) about which birth control method is right for her. If you have a son, talk to him about the responsibility he has to himself and to his partner (and future partners). Of course, birth control is only one aspect of safe sex, as we will discuss in the next section.

STIs

Unfortunately, what happens at college doesn't always stay at college. Some students leave their alma mater with more than just a diploma—they leave with an STI, a sometimes-permanent reminder of a poor decision. You may remember these infections as VD or STDs. Today they're called sexually transmitted infections, or STIs. Examples include chlamydia, HPV, HIV, syphilis, and genital herpes.

While it's easy to blame the hookup lifestyle for the spread of STIs on campuses, lack of education could also be to blame. Myths about STIs and sex abound.

The National College Health Assessment survey found that 54 percent of college students consistently use condoms during intercourse, but only 4 percent use condoms during oral sex. Many students believe oral sex is not actually "sex" and therefore that it can't lead to STIs. To make matters worse, many students believe STIs are always detectable to the naked eye. Not so. HPV, the most common STI in the country, often presents with no visible symptoms, although it can cause genital warts and cervical cancer if left untreated.

Practicing safer sex (using condoms and dental dams every time) will reduce, but not completely eliminate, the chances of contracting an STI. And every time means *every time*—even late on a Saturday night after a few too many Coors Lights. But the fact is, getting buzzed up on booze makes students less likely to practice safer sex, which increases their risks for STIs.

Sexually active students should be tested regularly and be aware of their partner's sexual history and current STI status. Students can struggle to make smart decisions, especially if they feel embarrassed broaching the topic with their partner. Talking about STIs is often awkward, however, knowledge is a crucial part of practicing safer sex. Model healthy communication by introducing the topic with your student.

Sexual Assault: When Sex Is Not a Choice

Not all sex on campus is consensual sex. Sexual assault is the broad term to describe a wide range of forced and unwanted sexual activity, including nonconsensual kissing, exhibitionism, groping, and rape. Victims may be coerced into sexual acts through verbal or nonverbal threats or through the use of alcohol or drugs.

One in six college women will experience rape or attempted rape. First-year women are the most vulnerable, with most rape attempts occurring within the first six weeks of college. Approximately four out of five sexual assaults are committed by an attacker the victim knows, according to the Rape, Abuse, and Incest National Network (RAINN). The majority—68 percent—of sexual assault incidents go unreported. The reasons for this are varied and complicated: social stigmas, fear of retaliation, distrust of authorities, and fear of blame.

These are sobering statistics for parents already fearful of sending children off to experience life on a college campus.

To protect themselves and the people they date, college students need to understand fundamental information about the line between consensual fun and assault. As shocking as this may sound, not everyone understands that distinction. This issue comes up regularly on campus disciplinary review boards across the nation. Students who thought they were just having fun realized (too late for both parties) that their behavior was actually sexual assault.

Consent is the key factor in any and every sexual activity. Consent isn't sexy. Consent is *necessary*.

The legal definition of consent varies from state to state, so be sure your student knows and understands the definition of consent for the state in which he or she attends college. Many states have adopted affirmative consent policies, requiring students on campuses to get permission at every stage of a sexual encounter. According to the National Center for Higher Education Risk Management, roughly fourteen hundred higher education institutions now use some type of "yes means yes" standard in their sexual assault policies. This means consent is never implied and cannot be assumed.

We understand "no means no," but affirmative consent says the absence of no does *not* mean yes. For example, when a student receives sexual advances but is highly intoxicated, he or she may be unable to say either yes or no to any sexual activity. Under the "yes means yes" standard, this inability to say yes, or to consent, automatically means no.

Affirmative consent policies are designed to help prevent wrong assumptions of consent. Unfortunately, though, sexual assaults still occur on campuses. If your child confides in you that he or she has been the victim of sexual assault, please understand it has taken a lot of courage to speak up. Try to keep your emotions (there will be many) in check. Listen without judging or immediately giving advice. More than anything, believe your child. Here's how to take care of your child's immediate needs.

Sexual Assault Guidelines

- Urge her (or him) to find a safe place and call 911. The earlier medical attention is sought, the better—for the quality of evidence collected and greater effectiveness of emergency contraception.

- Instruct her not to shower or bathe, douche, change clothes, or clean up. As counterintuitive as this sounds, this helps preserve evidence until a professional health care provider can examine the victim.

- Call or have her call someone she trusts—a friend, mentor, or counselor—to offer support and assistance.

- Have the trusted individual accompany her to the emergency room and stay with her for the duration of the visit. Emergency rooms are staffed around-the-clock with trained professionals, including psychological counselors and nurses with expertise in evidence collection. Beyond providing medical care for injuries, emergency rooms are also able to provide STI testing, antibiotic injections, and emergency contraception.

- Support her and encourage her to report it to the university and authorities.

- Encourage the victim to get professional counseling. Most colleges have an online list of services (counseling, health, and legal) available to both parents and students. She can also call the National Sexual Assault Hotline or contact RAINN for 24-7 guidance and support.
  National Sexual Assault Hotline: 800-656-HOPE (4673)
  RAINN: www.rainn.org

While not all assaults can be prevented, teach your student to protect him- or herself. Before your child leaves for school, have a serious heart-to-heart conversation about consent, risks, prevention, and what to do if your child (or a friend) is a victim.

This discussion can come on the heels of your talk about the risks of using alcohol or drugs, as the issues are often related. Justice Department data shows that alcohol- and drug-facilitated rape is one of the most commonly reported sexual assault crimes. And according to the National Institutes of Health, at least half of sexual assaults involve the consumption of alcohol by the perpetrator, the victim, or both.

Here are some discussion points to help you communicate with your student about sexual assault prevention:

Protect yourself. Learn self-defense. Many colleges or local police departments offer courses in basic self-defense. Carry a rape whistle.

Limit alcohol. Intoxication makes students more vulnerable to assaults by impairing judgment and/or inhibiting physical ability to fight off an attacker. As stated above, half of assaults involve alcohol.

Protect your drink. If your student chooses to drink, make sure she follows the rules of drinking smart described earlier in the chapter. Instruct your student to never accept a drink from someone else or from a communal alcohol source, such as a punch bowl. Your student should never leave a drink unattended, even to run to the restroom. This opens up an opportunity for someone to spike the drink with a date rape drug.

Stick together. Tell your student it's vital to attend social gatherings with a group of trusted friends who will look out for each other and help each other arrive home safely. When your student must venture alone, have her always tell someone where she's going, and urge her to avoid walking in unlit parts of campus. (Refer back to the safety section earlier in the chapter.)

Trust red flags. A bad feeling about a location or a person is a red flag. Teach your child to trust her instincts and leave if something doesn't seem right. If another person is making her uncomfortable, she should make some noise and draw attention to the situation.

Unwanted sexual activity can take an immeasurable toll on the victim's physical and mental health. The emotional and physical scars can deeply impact a student's ability to cope with academic, social, and personal responsibilities.

It is important for you to also understand how this incident affects you as a parent. Any feelings you may experience are normal and real. You'll likely want to seek professional counseling as well.

Eating Disorders

The transition into college life affects each student differently. For some, it's relatively smooth sailing. For others, the anxiety, social pressures, and competition can trigger an eating disorder as a way to cope with these stressors and perceived lack of control. With eating disorders, a student's relationship with food and body image can become distorted. Unfortunately, body image issues are already prevalent among this age group, making students even more susceptible to distorted thinking. Eating disorders can seriously affect overall health and well-being and cause emotional and academic challenges.

Heather, for example, was a straight-A student in high school and thrilled to be attending college out-of-state on a swimming scholarship. She aspired to get into law school, and she made friends easily.

In spite of her athleticism, Heather did not have a healthy body image. She would pore over magazines, then look in the mirror and get frustrated about her "baby fat." She'd make salads in the cafeteria but barely eat, pushing the lettuce around the plate. Her intense, twice-a-day workouts were depleting her body.

When she flew home for Thanksgiving, her parents were shocked at her appearance. "She was so thin—just skin and bones," says her mother. They knew immediately something was terribly wrong. Over the longer winter holiday break, they scheduled an appointment with a psychologist who specialized in eating disorders and fortunately got her on track for recovery.

Eating disorders are serious and often life threatening. They can affect both men and women. People suffering from eating disorders may be underweight, overweight, or somewhere in the middle. The disorders can take the form of:

- **Anorexia nervosa:** The student doesn't eat enough to maintain a healthy body weight.

- **Binge eating:** The student eats large amounts of food in a short period of time.

- **Bulimia:** The student binges and then purges either by forced vomiting, laxative use, or excessive exercising.

- **Muscle dysmorphia:** The student is obsessive about food, exercise, and supplements.

If you suspect your child is suffering from an eating disorder, respectfully share your concerns. Explain how much you care and why you're concerned. Share details about behaviors you've noticed. Be objective, calm, and nonjudgmental when discussing these behaviors. While they may seem completely irrational to you, this is painful and real for your child.

Eating disorders are not easy to fix, but professional therapy, nutritional counseling, and medical care will help. The earlier a student gets proper treatment, the better his chances of a timely, effective recovery.

Anxiety and Depression

College can be stressful. Students must juggle school, work, friends, and finances, all while trying to figure out the trajectory of the rest of their lives. Feelings of loneliness and isolation can overwhelm even the most well-prepared students.

Anxiety has now surpassed depression as the most common mental health diagnosis among college students, though depression too is creeping up. According to the annual national survey by the American College Health Association, nearly one in six college students has been diagnosed with or treated for anxiety within the last twelve months. More than half of students who visit campus clinics cite anxiety as a health concern, according to a study of more than 100,000 students nationwide by the Center for Collegiate Mental Health at Penn State.

Anxiety is an umbrella term for several disorders and can accompany many other diagnoses, such as depression. While causes vary and are often hard to identify, academic pressures, previous traumas, overprotective parents, and genetics have been linked to increased anxiety in students. Feeling depressed is a fairly common occurrence among college students who are living on their own for the first time.

Even social media plays a role in anxiety and depression. Readily available at their fingertips 24-7, social media is a double-edged sword that can quickly slice through self-esteem. As students view posts about everyone else's "fabulous" lives, the inevitable internal comparisons trick already fragile, stressed-out minds.

At this age, students are still maturing and developing the coping skills to manage their perfect storm of emotions. Kimberly Christensen, PsyD, a pediatric psychologist, reminds parents there is a typical adjustment to college for all students. "There's excitement and stress, so keep that in mind," she says. "Even a child who is depressed may be just stressed by college, and some of that stress is good. Parents need to tease out what's depression and what's typical stress."

For many students, time and self-help are enough to pull through a "low" time. However, other students have more severe feelings of depression or anxiety. In these cases, professional evaluation and medical treatment may be necessary.

Both anxiety and depression can be persistent and incapacitating. Many students don't seek treatment because they don't even realize the seriousness of their situation. They may be embarrassed, they may view their feelings as personal weakness, or they may feel too "stuck" to reach out.

Signs of anxiety and depression are varied and often hard for parents to catch, especially when children attend college far from home. It's difficult to decide over the phone if she's just having a bad day or if she's truly struggling. But here are some signs that your student may need help:

- Negative feelings that persist for several weeks

- Irritability

- Forgetfulness

- Lack of motivation, missing class, procrastination

- Sleep disturbances, difficulty waking up

- Lingering, unidentified illnesses

- Loss of interest in usual activities

- Rapid weight loss or gain

- Difficulties with alcohol or other drugs

Is your student feeling overwhelmed and out of control? It may be time to suggest a visit with a counselor. Counseling—as well as exercise, good nutrition, and adequate sleep—is a healthy choice for a stressed-out student.

If you're concerned and feel your child needs to talk with somebody, the campus counseling center is a good place to start. Counseling centers provide mental health services for current students. Licensed professionals are available for confidential consultations and can refer students for further help. Some centers offer drop-in sessions that teach stress-relieving techniques. Others even bring therapy dogs onsite for some furry stress relief during finals.

Some students are already under a physician's care to manage depression or anxiety prior to attending college. If your student is already taking a prescribed antidepressant, reiterate the importance of her staying on the prescribed meds. Also discuss the danger of medications interacting with alcohol or other substances.

Different students have different needs, especially those with mental health issues. How much and in what ways you help your student will vary. If your child has depression or anxiety, your role as a parent and mentor is a key part of his freshman voyage.

"People are so worried these days about being a helicopter parent. But in my experience, it's totally appropriate to have regular contact with your child," Christensen says. "Regularly call or text or check in on certain days or times. Ask how things are going, how they're eating, if they're exercising, what they're doing on weekends. Those questions can help parents who are pretty in tune with their kids tell if something is going on. Communication really shouldn't be any different for kids who have depression."

Suicide

As we've reiterated, a student will experience a wide range of emotions when he goes off to school. He will be excited, anxious, scared, happy, sad—all of which are normal. An important part of a college education is encountering intellectual, personal, emotional, and social challenges. These challenges all create varying levels of stress.

However, when the stressors exceed a student's coping abilities, such as if he's already struggling with depression or anxiety, his risk factors for suicide rise. And suicide risk is nothing to take lightly. In fact, suicide is the third-leading cause of death among people between the ages of fifteen and twenty-four. It is something we parents worry about and simply cannot ignore.

If you notice the following changes—red flags—in your student, be aware that they could indicate suicidal thoughts.

Changes in Mood
- Agitation or increased anxiety, crying often

- Rage or anger

- Depression

- Sudden mood swings

Changes in Performance and Focus

- Distracted or preoccupied

- Drop in grades

- Skipping or missing classes

Changes in Behavior and Social Interaction

- Withdrawing from friends and family

- Increased high-risk behaviors

- Change in sleep patterns (sleeping excessively or having insomnia)

- Stays in room (or in bed) much of the time

Changes in Appearance

- Disheveled

- Poor hygiene

- Sudden weight loss or gain

Changes in Outlook

- Helplessness

- Hopelessness

- Making comments such as "What's the point in trying?"

Parents, you likely know your child better than anyone. If you are concerned about suicide, ask her about suicide directly.

Now is not the time to sugarcoat the conversation nor to dive into denial. Be specific with the reasons for your concerns, and provide examples of the changes you have noticed in her behavior, mood, appearance, or outlook.

Then listen to her responses. Even though your thoughts will be racing from one extreme to another, show compassion and avoid criticizing or judging. And do not minimize her feelings with "You're just stressed out" or "You just need to relax—it'll get better." Even though these are well-meaning comments, they are not helpful. They don't give your student the sense you actually understand her. Rather, it may help to paraphrase what you hear her say to show that you are really listening.

If You Suspect Your Child Is Suicidal:

- Have a compassionate, private conversation.

- Be direct—ask if she's thinking about suicide.

- Focus on specific behaviors—e.g., changes in mood, performance, behavior.

- Take what is said seriously. Listen without criticizing or judging the behaviors.

- Do not promise to keep what is said a secret. Your goal is to get help for your child, which may require turning to outside professionals.

Once you have a pulse on where she is emotionally and mentally, you can offer support and guide her toward help. If the risk of your child harming herself is not immediate, you can start by contacting the National Suicide Prevention Lifeline at suicidepreventionlifeline.org. You may also want to contact your student's campus counseling center for professional advice. These mental health care professionals are trained to handle crisis situations—specifically those of college students.

However, sometimes immediate action is required. If your child expresses a desire to hurt or kill herself, and/or if she has access to a means of suicide (such as a gun or pills), seek help immediately.

To Seek Immediate Help

- DO NOT leave your child alone.

- Call campus police or 911 and tell the dispatcher your child is a danger to herself.

- Contact a crisis center helpline. They are answered immediately by trained crisis intervention specialists.

  - **National Suicide Prevention Lifeline**: 800-273-TALK (8255)

  - **National Suicide Prevention Text Crisis Line**: 741741

Sometimes it isn't your child who is struggling but his roommate or friend. If your student comes to you with concerns about a friend or roommate exhibiting suicidal red flags, you can guide him through options for helping.

First, you may want to suggest your child contact the campus counseling center. They are there to support the struggling student as well as the concerned friend. Your student could also bring up his concerns with an RA or housing director. Both are trained in crisis management and know available resources on campus.

In any case, urge your child to seek help for his friend one way or another. Often students shy away from reaching out to professional resources because they're afraid of being "wrong" if the friend is not suicidal after all. However, remind your student that red flags are red flags for a reason. Even if it turns out the friend is not suicidal, the warning signs could also indicate problems related to depression, drugs or alcohol, or sexual assault—all of which require professional care.

Lastly, your student can choose to have a caring, private conversation with the friend about his concerns. If your child is willing to step in and assist a friend or roommate in crisis, be sure he understands that taking care of himself is his first responsibility. He cannot sacrifice his own well-being in the process of caring for a friend.

As a parent-mentor, you'll want to offer support to your student if he chooses this route. It is often scary and stressful to approach this tender subject—especially with a friend or roommate. Remind your student that it is not his role to solve his friend's problems, but talking with his friend will show that he cares and that his friend is not alone. Also, assure him that talking about suicide will not "push" the friend to commit suicide. The conversation guidelines and emergency instructions listed above for parent-to-student situations apply in student-to-student situations as well.

Suicide is a serious issue affecting today's young people. The freshman voyage, especially, can be a rough passage. Do not assume your child and her friends are "fine" and that suicide would "never" be a worry. Before your child leaves for school, arm her with resources such as the hotlines and support organizations listed above. It could be a lifeline for your student or one of her friends.

Illness

The stomach flu. Mono. Sinus infections. Yes, big kids still get sick—especially at college. In fact, students will push their immune systems to the limit with little sleep, poor nutrition, and dehydration, then wonder why they get sick. With close quarters and not-so-smart choices, they share their "bugs" with others. Achoo!

For eighteen years, your child has turned to you whenever she doesn't feel well. Don't be surprised when you get the call with her voice all hoarse and scratchy. As discussed in chapter 9, parents are usually first in the line of communication when something goes amiss.

Of course, it's tough to make chicken noodle soup and set up a cozy nest on the couch when she's miles away at sea. So when illness strikes, student health services come to the rescue. Direct your student to the campus clinic. These medical professionals can handle basic health care needs and provide a little TLC for students, usually at a reduced cost from traditional medical clinics.

To help your child prevent illness in the first place, encourage her to be smart about handwashing and sharing germs, though it's often hard to avoid swapping bugs when living in tight quarters. To support her immune system and promote overall health, she should eat nutritious meals (it's possible even in the dorm cafeteria), exercise regularly, and get plenty of rest. Of these, rest is particularly important and often overlooked.

A consistent, balanced sleep schedule is one of the best mental and physical health enhancers available, yet most college students do not get enough sleep. Often students are unaware that their sleep deprivation—which is usually self-inflicted for academic or social reasons—can cause serious problems.

So parents, while we can't make them sleep, we can let them know how much we love them and want them to be healthy. We can remind them that sleep is a critical piece of maintaining both physical and mental health. While it might not always work, it can't hurt if dear old dad gives a gentle reminder to make rest a priority.

Note, however, that your child's health and counseling service records are subject to even more confidentiality restrictions than his educational records are. You will not be notified if your student schedules an appointment. College officials and medical staff recognize that confidentially allows students to talk openly and candidly with medical staff without fear the information will be shared with others—even (or, in some occasions, especially) parents. It's yet another way the balance of responsibility shifts from parents to students.

That said, in the event of a potentially life-threatening emergency, universities are able to contact parents or guardians without prior consent from the student. Most colleges have emergency notification policies in place for this type of situation. If a hospital or law enforcement agency is involved, they will have their own notification protocols.

Spring Break

Cancun. Aruba. Jamaica. South Padre. Daytona Beach. When your student starts talking about spring break, these warm-weather destinations will sound like wonderful respites from the stressors of college life. She'll tell you about her plans to "just chill out" on the beach with friends. She'll pluck at your heartstrings (and your wallet) telling you warm sand, sunshine, and relaxation are all she wants after studying so hard all year.

While she's selling you on a girls' getaway that includes a catamaran snorkel cruise and a great rate at an all-inclusive resort, you'll want to do a little research of your own before supporting this endeavor. Some destinations will likely be as low-key as she describes. But for certain destinations—the popular ones—you may not be getting the full story.

Unfortunately, the full story is scary—the stuff parental night-mares are made of. A simple Google search will reveal fight-filled, booze-filled, chaotic beaches with incoherent students passed out on the sand. The CNN and Fox News Insider sites share story after story of alcohol, drugs, crime, theft, and uninhibited sex on the beach.

One student described witnessing a couple having intercourse while the crowd watched and cheered. Florida made headlines in 2015 after a nineteen-year-old woman was captured on video while being gang raped on a crowded stretch of Panama City Beach. Another report describes a group of people, nicknamed 100-milers, who travel miles to spring break destinations with the sole purpose of preying on college students. These predators drug, rob, and violate students.

Does spring break still sound like a good idea for your child? Instead of a chill getaway, you could be sending your student off on an all-expense-paid *Girls Gone Wild* booze cruise to STI land—or worse.

If you decline to fund a frolic on the beach this spring break, let him down gently but firmly. If your reasons are financial, share that reality. College-aged adults need to understand that money doesn't grow on trees. They need to be taught that it's not prudent to take out a bank loan to pay for a spring break vacation.

If your reasons are moral or safety related, share them as well. When he argues that "everybody's going but me," you can assure him you only want what's best for him. Will he like it? Of course not. Will he push back? Absolutely.

Once he gives up the crusade and accepts reality, offer some spring break alternatives for him to consider. While none of these options provide the sun-kissed skin he's hoping for, they are safer, more pocketbook-friendly alternatives to a traditional spring break. No nasty videos, beer bongs, or bank loans required. (As most of these options involve the student coming home, be sure to check out chapter 14 next. That's where we'll discuss the ups and downs of students returning to home port after being out to sea.)

7 Alternatives to Partying over Spring Break

1. **Bring the gang home.** If your student was really looking forward to spending some time with his buds, encourage him to bring the buds home over break. Bribe them with home cooking, lots of rest, and two-ply toilet paper. This is a fantastic way for you to get to know the friends in his life. Have him show them the interesting things his hometown has to offer—or just let him run a nonstop gaming marathon in the basement.

2. **Volunteer.** By volunteering, your student can make a difference and build a resume at the same time. Not sure where to start? Have her look into nursing homes, food banks, places of worship, or animal shelters. Serving others can give your student perspective and humility—wonderful character qualities that help young adults grow and mature.

3. **Get a (summer) job.** Applying for summer jobs and internships now, before the rush of applicants at the end of the semester, can give your student a leg up on the competition. If he's looking at an opportunity in your hometown, spring break is a great time to schedule a face-to-face interview.

4. **Work.** Yes, actually work. Why not make money rather than hemorrhage money over spring break? If your student doesn't have a job, consider negotiating pay for those odd jobs that never seem to get done at home. Muck out the garage. Paint the hallway. Scrub the porch.

Rake the lawn. It's money in the bank for your student and money well spent for you. At last you can check a few items off the honey-do list.

5. **Enjoy family time.** Dorothy was on to something when she said "There's no place like home." Spending spring break with the fam gives your student a chance to reconnect. What a perfect opportunity for some relaxed family time together. (Again, see chapter 14 about setting realistic expectations.) And if your student is lucky enough to have grandparents still living, why not plan a visit? Your child will one day look back and appreciate the gift of time with Grandma, even if it's not be the tropical getaway she was hoping for. (Unless, of course, Grandma lives someplace warm herself.)

6. **Research careers.** Suggest your student use spring break as a chance to shadow a professional in a field of interest. It's like getting a sneak peek on a potential career path. Not only will he observe a day in the life for the career but he may also make professional connections for future referrals or internship opportunities.

7. **Self-care.** Treat spring break as spa week for your student's soul. After countless cafeteria meals, she can enjoy delicious, healthy homemade meals. After the chaos of the dorms, she can take full advantage of quiet spaces to catch up on rest. She can make time to exercise and practice self-care—even schedule that past-due dental or eye appointment and haircut. She'll go back to school refreshed and ready to finish out the year.

Man Overboard—When (and How) to Intervene

As this chapter suggests, we cannot disaster-proof our kids—no matter how much we want to. While we want to Bubble Wrap them, we can't protect them from every bump, bruise, or danger they'll encounter. Most of these experiences ultimately become beneficial lessons, as we've discussed throughout the book. We must remember: a smooth sea never made a skilled sailor.

There may come a time, however, when your child goes overboard and needs a lifeline—when parental action is completely appropriate and necessary. If your child is suicidal or self-harming, absolutely you should make a call for intervention. If alcohol or drugs are negatively affecting his life, that's another time. If he's failing out of school, you must guide him to seek professional help.

What can you do when you realize your child is seriously struggling and needs help? Contact the college counseling center, the office of student affairs, or the dean of students for guidance. They care about your student's safety, well-being, and success.

If you contact the office of the dean, the staff will talk with you about your concerns as well as talk about strategies for addressing them. Ideally, though, you should also plan to have the same conversation with your student. With open lines of communication, you can partner with the university to be the support your child needs to get back on course. Dr. Cara Halgren, University of North Dakota associate vice president and dean of students, explains:

> We can be most helpful in situations where parents are willing to have conversations with their students about their concerns as well as share with them that they have consulted us for help. This gives us a clear path to work with the students and parents together.

221

At times, we have parents call us who want help—but that don't want their student to know they called us. We can still be of assistance, but it is limited given the boundaries placed on us.

As we've mentioned, privacy laws prevent many professionals from sharing details with you about your student. But that doesn't mean you, as a parent, can't call the university and make them aware of a situation. For example, a clinic cannot acknowledge whether your student is a patient, but you can inform them of your concern that your student shows signs of depression. They have the training and expertise to connect your student with the appropriate resources, and they can provide you, the parents, with support as you address the scary stuff you can't ignore.

As Dr. Halgren states, "I always tell parents that no one knows their student better than they do. No one. So I urge them to call us and talk through their concerns whenever they have that parent 'gut' response that tells them something isn't right."

Empower Yourself, Empower Your Student

I realize this chapter only touches the surface of the scary stuff we can't ignore. Hopefully it offers a basic understanding of the many challenges our students face, the many tsunamis that can overtake them.

Let me reiterate: my intent is not to scare you or to cause more sleepless nights but to empower you with resources and information when the going gets tough. A strong knowledge base along with common sense and good communication will help you in turn empower your student to make healthy, safe choices during the college years—and beyond.

PART

THREE

BACK IN PORT

FOURTEEN

WHEN THE SHIP RETURNS

Sailing a boat calls for quick action, a blending of feeling with the wind and water as well as with the very heart and soul of the boat itself. Sailing teaches alertness and courage, and gives in return a joyousness and peace that but few sports afford.
—GEORGE MATTHEW ADAMS

Doesn't move-in day seem like yesterday—yet also feel like a lifetime ago? When your child is out to sea during the freshman year, time both flies and crawls.

But before you know it, your sailor will be back in port. Winter break, holiday break, spring break, and then summer break—these are all opportunities for your child to return home on shore leave. And they're all opportunities for highs and lows you may not expect.

What to Expect over Break

1. Your child will come home tired. Expect him to sleep a lot.

2. Your child will come home hungry. Expect her to eat a lot.

3. Your child will come home with piles of dirty laundry. Expect your washing machine to run a lot.

4. Your child is used to having alone time. Expect his need for space.

5. Your child is also used to having social time. Expect her to want to see her friends.

6. Your child is self-sufficient and able to manage his own schedule. Expect him to want some autonomy.

7. Your child will come home eager to let you know how smart, evolved, and worldly she has become. Expect to be challenged a lot.

Get the gist? Good. Now let's discuss shore leave in more detail.

The First Break

The first semester is a time of great change for college students. Winter or holiday break is often the longest stretch when the student returns home. For some students, it's the first time home at all. Whether your child has been home several prior weekends or whether you haven't seen her since move-in day, be prepared for a change on break.

I waited with anticipation for our daughter to arrive home for winter break. I'd been envisioning a Norman Rockwell Christmas in my head for weeks. We'd relish in five weeks of blissful togetherness. All of us under the same roof eating popcorn, watching movies, sharing stories, feeling the love. We would delight in listening to all the details of Brooke's new collegiate life and just enjoy spending time as a family.

Then she came home. She blew in like a hurricane and dropped what appeared to be six weeks' worth of laundry in the mud room. After a hug and a kiss, she retreated to her bedroom to unpack. I found her there, sound asleep, four hours later.

The first week was wonderful. Hugs, meals together, and holiday cheer. The second week was pleasant. She bubbled over with gratitude for the little things: home-cooked meals, a queen-sized bed, bubble baths, and two-ply toilet paper.

It all changed during week three. That's when the conflicts began. A snarky I'm-eighteen-and-in-college-and-too-smart-for-you attitude appeared out of nowhere. My defensive instincts kicked in. I wanted to feed humble pie to this budding adult.

Fortunately, though, I had a flashback to 1988. I remembered a big-haired, bright-eyed college freshman home for her first long break. I recalled the conflicts, the seemingly incessant nagging of parents, and the desire to show everybody how much I'd learned and matured.

This flashback-turned-reality-check gave me some much needed perspective and a boost in maternal patience. I had to remember Brooke was teetering on the narrow gangplank between childhood and adulthood.

Our daughter was now that bright-eyed young woman who wanted to let us know she was not the same girl who'd left on move-in day. She was, in fact, growing and maturing and stretching her brain to accommodate new ideas and new ways of thinking.

Once I recognized this, I was able to relax and listen. I could appreciate (most of) her new philosophies and broadened ideas.

We engaged in some stimulating conversations. It was in those moments that I caught a glimpse of the confident, responsible, thoughtful woman she was becoming.

While each student evolves in her own way, parents often see notable changes during the long holiday break. Most students are eager to assert their newly found independence and share their broadened perspectives. After all, they've spent the past months meeting new people and learning about lifestyles, upbringing, and perspectives different from their own.

As a parent, try to listen to your student with an open mind, even if you don't agree with what's being said. It's not easy, but it will open doors to further conversation and let your student know you value her opinion. It will help set the tone for future visits home as well.

The Disappearing Act

Sometimes the hardest part about your child being home on break is that he doesn't seem to be home at all. In fact, this disappearing act is quite common, especially among first-year college students.

Lori lamented about how she saw her son for about twenty minutes of his twenty-day break. "He came home to sleep, eat, and shower," she complained. "That's it." Otherwise he was out socializing with his high school friends.

First-year students on break are eager to get together with their friends to reminisce and swap stories. Often, this socializing includes alcohol, which can be a rude awakening for many parents when their child comes home under the influence—or doesn't come home at all. Drinking or no drinking, friends seem to have more pull than family.

Christine, a freshman mom, expressed her disappointment in her daughter's first visit home from college for Thanksgiving. "At the airport, my daughter ran into my arms and burst into tears telling me how happy she was to be home. But then she spent 90 percent of the holiday with her boyfriend and friends from high school. I did tell her that I was disappointed we didn't get to spend much time together and that I expected her to make more time at Christmas for me and my hubby, her dad. But I don't want to force it."

What's a parent to do? How do we establish realistic boundaries and expectations with our college students?

Another mom, Lauren, offers a solution and shares her joy at how the first holiday home went for her family.

I drove our freshman son and his friend to the airport yesterday afternoon, to fly back to school across the country. He's our oldest, so this was our first Thanksgiving with a college kid! They were here for a full week, and it exceeded my expectations.

I think part of it was that I set expectations for them before they got here about when we expected them to be with us and when they had free time—which they were free to spend with us! That really helped, as there was no guilting anyone into spending time together.

I also loved seeing how close my son was with the friend (and rowing teammate) that he brought home. He said at one point over the weekend, 'I am making lifetime friends there. Not four-year friends, but lifetime friends.' I loved that and could see it with how close he and this young man are. It makes me feel good that three thousand miles away, he has people whose back he will watch and who will watch his! Can't wait to see him in twenty-two days!

I think Lauren nailed it. She and her son discussed scheduling expectations prior to his flight home. That way, they experienced no conflict or guilt-trips over schedules. Lauren was realistic and understood her son's need to see his friends, and he understood her need to have him participate in some family activities. He felt validated and involved in the decision-making process.

For those who don't get a chance to talk ahead of time, seasoned parents suggest sitting down to lay out the new house rules right after your child arrives home—before the friends start calling. For example, while she likely no longer has an established curfew, she is expected to send a courtesy text if she'll be out after midnight. Or she's expected to honor tradition and participate in particular holiday family gatherings.

It never hurts to remind your student that family living requires mutual respect and some give-and-take from both parents and children. Then, as parent-mentors, we must also remember to heed our own advice. We must give up a little control and respect our budding adults.

Sibling Transition

Younger siblings experience mixed emotions when the college student returns. While likely eager to have big bro home, a younger sib can also feel displaced. The college student receives a welcome fit for a king—his favorite meals, visits with friends, freedom to stay out until the wee hours, and everyone's attention. The younger sibling can feel lost—even invisible—as she sees the college student monopolizing family time and resources.

Both siblings have grown and changed in the weeks since move-in day. Depending on the age spread, the younger child may be confused by the college student's changes—whether real or perceived. The siblings may need a little time to become reacquainted and find their face-to-face groove again.

It's easy, as parents, to force this process and "make" them spend time together. But try to refrain from this, as it often backfires. Be careful not to plunk a parental guilt-trip on the returning student if she wants to spend time with friends or even alone, rather than hang out with the little sis. Also recognize that the younger sibling has likely become comfortable with her new role in the pecking order. Readjusting to the family hierarchy will take some time for the entire family.

Open, honest conversation before the college student returns can assist in the transition. Talk with each of your children about how college experiences can change perspectives and alter relationships, including their relationships with each other. Remind them each of the importance of patience and communication.

Summer Break—It's No Picnic

With rose-colored glasses planted firmly on the bridge of my nose, I counted the days until my baby would return home for the summer. I'd conveniently forgotten any Christmastime conflicts.

Wise friends urged cautious optimism, but I refused to listen. Several experienced mothers warned me—unsuccessfully—about the dreaded first-summer-home-from-college syndrome. "Oh, honey," one friend sighed. "Just know it won't be easy." They bared their maternal souls, sharing horror stories about rude, ungrateful offspring returning home from their first year of university life.

So when our firstborn made it home for her three-month summer break, I was over the moon as the first two weeks passed without a hitch. No nasty attitude. No late-night parties. No rude, condescending, know-it-all comments to the "little people" back home. It was smooth sailing.

Until week three.

Then the novelty of being home once again wore off. Her appreciation of home-cooked meals and the pleasure of showering without flip-flops didn't sustain the honeymoon phase of our summer together. Her annoyed eye rolls at the sound of my voice and constant irritation at her younger sister replaced the hugs and thank-yous of the first two weeks.

Then little things began to irritate me too. A lot. For example, apparently you never ever turn a light switch off at college. After she'd leave for work, I'd have to run around the house turning off lights in nearly every room she'd entered that morning. We spent eighteen years training her to conserve energy and save money, using generations-old parental gems such as, "Turn off the lights! We don't own the electric company!" To make room for all her educational opportunities that first year of college, she appeared to forget a lifetime of household training.

There was more. After having somebody behind the cafeteria counter washing her dishes, she somehow forgot how to open our dishwasher and place her dirty dishes inside. She could simultaneously "talk" to twenty-four people between Facebook, texting, Twitter, Snapchat, and Instagram, yet she was unable to place her dirty socks and underwear in her clothes hamper.

As a mom quickly running out of patience with the fruit of my loins, I had to force myself to remember she'd been on her own for nearly a year and had gained a lot of independence. While the growing laundry pile on her bathroom floor and her inability to open the dishwasher might have suggested otherwise, I knew deep down this seemingly spoiled princess was still my hardworking, deep-feeling daughter. I knew without a doubt she'd been in many new (possibly uncomfortable) situations in the past year and had likely matured in ways I had yet to grasp.

So instead of labeling her with all the nasty names bubbling in my brain, I sat down to discuss it woman to woman. I told her I needed her to step up and pitch in like an adult.

I'm happy to say, she did eventually remember how to use the dishwasher. She even occasionally got on the business end of the vacuum cleaner. But I had to lower my standards regarding that mound of clothes propagating on her bathroom floor.

I'm a firm believer in parents being parents and kids understanding that living under our roof means they are required to follow certain house rules. That being said, we parents do need to put on our mentoring hats even during summer break. We need to understand it's tough for kids coming home to live under our rules when they've been running their own schedules without guidance all year.

One expert says parents may not see the maturity of their kids when they come home their first summer because kids tend to regress back to their old high school ways. After being forced to practice self-discipline while at college, they let loose and relax in the comfort of home.

His suggestion? Even if your child returns to his seventeen-year-old ways, don't regress to that stage yourself. Attempt to give him the independence and responsibility he had while away at school. In return, he may be encouraged to show you just how much he has actually matured.

In those moments when you're connecting over break (i.e., when your child is physically present, conscious, and actually in the mood to talk), make a pot of coffee and start a conversation using some of the ideas below. Then sit back and listen.

Remember—summer break isn't forever. Hope for the best, but be prepared for the worst. Practice patience. Enjoy your child, because her breaks back home are numbered. One day, you might actually miss that pile of clothing on the bathroom floor.

Summer Break Conversation Starters

1. Was your first year what you expected? Why? Why not?

2. Who was your favorite professor? Why?

3. What was your favorite/least favorite class? Why?

4. Tell me about the people on your floor. How did you meet them?

5. Did you join any clubs or organizations? Tell me about them.

6. Where was your favorite place to study? Why?

7. How did you feel about your course load? Were you able to balance the amount of work?

8. What are your hopes for next year?

PART

FOUR

REFLECTING ON THE VOYAGE

FIFTEEN

A LETTER FROM MOM

Oh, what a journey, this letting go! From diapers to diplomas, we do our best. We invest our time and our souls into our offspring. We kiss boo-boos and read *I'll Love You Forever* and *Oh, The Places You'll Go!* We attend band concerts, scout meetings, and parent-teacher conferences. We instill values and teach character.

We celebrate the things that make our children unique and wonderful. We laugh with them and cry with them. Sometimes we even cry for them.

We endure sleepless nights, papier-mâche elephants, swimming lessons, and broken curfews. We keep them as safe as we can, clinging to their little hands and teaching them to look both ways before crossing the street.

And then it happens. They grow up. They let go. And so must we.

Below is the letter I left on our daughter's pillow on her freshman move-in day. The day I clung to my husband's hand and barely made it across the street to the parking lot. The day I chose to let go and allow her to embark on her voyage into adulthood. The day that made me proud and tore my heart to shreds at the same time.

The letter offered the words I could not speak but I felt needed to be said. Even now, nearly two years later, I tear up when I read them. The emotions of that season still swell within me. But they're a part of my story, her voyage, our lives.

What could my words possibly mean to you? They're proof that you can—and will—survive this journey. You may ache. You may hit some turbulent waters. But you'll also find great joy in the moments of growth—yours and your child's—throughout the freshman voyage.

Dear Brooke,

As you head off to Drake this week, I am fighting mixed feelings. I know you're ready and eager to go. I want you to have this time, your college years, to evolve as the woman you will become. I really do. But another part of me—the clingy, terrified maternal part—wants to pull you close and not let go. I realize this is irrational, and I admit it. But rational or not, it is real. Always know you are loved and that I only want what is best for you. That is why I will let you go—no matter how much my instincts are fighting to grasp at fragments of the little girl I'm afraid to lose.

I can only imagine what your future may hold. But knowing you, it will be out-of-the-box. Whether through nature or nurture or necessity, you've developed a gift for tenacity and for seeking out your own path. Your open mind and love of people will serve you well.

So go. Go experience life. Embrace new people and new ideas. Please remember what a privilege it is to have this opportunity and make the most out of it. Take advantage of the resources and the freedoms that are unique to these years of your life. Study hard. Play hard. Work hard. College is about more than just academics.

A LETTER FROM MOM

As you go, please remain both humble and grateful. Not everybody gets to have this experience, so appreciate it. All of it. Even the crabby professors. The community bathrooms. The cafeteria food. You'll take away something from every aspect, both positive and negative. A grateful heart will help you be a gracious person.

Immerse yourself in your new environment, but please don't forget me. Call home once in a while just to let me know what's going on in your life. I may not be so shocked by what you'll share with me. I've likely already tried it myself. I may even have some useful insights to share with you, if you want them. In spite of my dinosaur status, remember that I was your age once. I was a vibrant, energetic, curious college student too. I've not forgotten the mixed emotions and the stressors. I remember the insecurities. And the fun. Baby, don't forget to have fun.

Nobody loves you more than I do. Nobody wants your success more than I do. I will always support you, but your future is up to you.
For now, I'll do my best to let you go.

Love,
Mom

APPENDIX A
WORDS OF AFFIRMATION

As mentioned in chapter 9, I'm a big believer in the day-brightening power of snail mail, especially when the message is positive and intentional. But please don't let this concept intimidate you. You don't have to be an English major to deliver a delightful message that inspires, comforts, and offers boatloads of support. In fact, I've made it easy for you to get rolling.

Below is a list of character qualities you can identify and affirm in your child. Just pick a word or two that describes your student and tell him why those words best fit him. If *enthusiastic* and *kindhearted* are your words of choice, perhaps write something such as this: "I've always admired your enthusiasm for helping others. I know this will open doors for you and help you meet other kindhearted people." A couple of sentences is all it takes to send your love and make his day!

For more inspiration, see appendix B for motivational quotes.

adaptable	bright	conscientious
adventurous	brilliant	considerate
ambitious	calm	cooperative
appreciative	candid	courageous
approachable	caring	creative
artistic	cheerful	curious
brave	compassionate	dependable

determined
devoted
diligent
disciplined
eager
easygoing
encouraging
energetic
enthusiastic
fair
faithful
forgiving
friendly
fun loving
funny
generous
gentle
giving
grateful
happy
hardworking
helpful
honest
humble
humorous
imaginative
independent
inspiring
integrity
intelligent
joyful
leader

logical
loving/lovable
loyal
mature
observant
optimistic
passionate
patient
perceptive
persistent
positive
proficient
reliable
resilient
respectful
responsible
self-confident
sincere
smart
spiritual
strong
studious
successful
talented
thoughtful
tolerant
trustworthy
unique
unselfish
wise
witty

APPENDIX B
QUOTES TO INSPIRE AND MOTIVATE

When reaching out via snail mail, sometimes it's easier to let someone else's words speak for you or at least inspire you. For a quick yet effective way to send some inspiration, select a quote below (or find one you like online), then write a couple of sentences about why you like it and how it relates to your student's current situation. For example:

Dear Junior,
Ann Landers once said, "Opportunities are usually disguised as hard work, so most people don't recognize them." I thought of you when I came across that quote. I hope it gives you some comfort and perspective as you work on that big paper for American lit. Even a lit paper can be an opportunity to learn how to express your viewpoint in a meaningful way. That skill will prove valuable wherever life leads you.
Love, Mom

So, select a quote, grab a pen and paper, and get started!

REFLECTING ON THE VOYAGE

Goals are dreams with deadlines.
—Diana Scharf Hunt

*Never give up, for that is just the place and time
that the tide will turn.*
—Harriet Beecher Stowe

The best project you'll ever work on is you.
—Author unknown

*Hardships often prepare ordinary people for an
extraordinary destiny.*
—C. S. Lewis

*Sometimes it is not enough to do our best; we must do
what is required.*
—Winston Churchill

New beginnings are often disguised as painful endings.
—Lao Tzu

*Where you are today is no accident.
God is using the situation you are in right now to shape
you and prepare you for the place
He wants to bring you into tomorrow.
Trust Him with His plan even if you don't understand it.*
—Author unknown

QUOTES TO INSPIRE AND MOTIVATE

Be yourself; everyone else is already taken.
—OSCAR WILDE

*Great works are performed not by strength
but by perseverance.*
—SAMUEL JOHNSON

*Perseverance is failing nineteen times
and succeeding the twentieth.*
—JULIE ANDREWS

*We are what we repeatedly do. Excellence, then,
is not an act, but a habit.*
—ARISTOTLE

*Character consists of what you do on the third
and fourth tries.*
—JAMES A. MICHENER

Success is outliving your failures.
—ERMA BOMBECK

*Most folks are about as happy as they make up
their minds to be.*
—ABRAHAM LINCOLN

APPENDIX C
Care Package Ideas

I know what you're thinking: *Care packages? Is my kid at college or summer camp?* (A legitimate question, of course. I made the college-to-camp comparison myself in chapter 7 about move-in day.)

But residence hall directors and RAs confirm that care packages really are a big deal in the dorms. "You should see them bound down to the desk once they receive a package notification," explains one hall director. "It is definitely a day brightener for the student, like sunshine in a shoe box."

Simply put, students appreciate care packages.

At its most fundamental, a care package is a sturdy box filled with a few of your child's favorite things or stuff he'd like. If you want to go a step further and create a themed care package, read on. I've put together several themes for you below. Just take this book along to Target or your nearest dollar or party store as a shopping checklist. There are ideas for both guys and girls.

Have fun with it! The more fun you have putting it together, the more fun your student will have opening it up.

We're Blue Without You

This care package is a great one for early in the school year. Just send anything blue.

Blue socks, T-shirt, or scarf

Blue nail polish

Blue Sharpie

Blue toothbrush

Shave gel (blue, of course)

Cleansing towelettes (Neutrogena has some in a blue package)

York Pieces peppermint candies (yes, they're blue and white)

Lysol Disinfectant Spray to Go (in a blue bottle, of course)

Peppermint breath mints

Favorite easy-to-prepare foods packaged in blue (Kraft Mac & Cheese, anyone?)

Aloha! A Day at the Beach

This island-themed package is a fun way to warm up a cold winter day. It could also work for a student unable to get away during spring break.

Leis (from the party store)

Sunscreen

Beach ball

Cheap sunglasses

Beach-themed photo frame

Lemonade mix

Goldfish crackers

Swedish Fish candy

Dried pineapple

Deodorant (the practical part of the package)

A new pair of flip-flops for the shower

It's All Greek to Me

If your child is in a fraternity or sorority, find out the organization's theme or special colors. For example, our daughter's sorority is represented by a kite and the colors black and gold. Their flower is a pansy. Knowing the themes and symbols makes for easy-to-assemble care packages. As another idea, most Greek organizations have websites filled with gift items you can order.

Greek letter T-shirt

Hand-decorated pillowcase

Lanyard or keychain

Notecards

Anything in the house colors

Birthday Party in a Box

Is your student celebrating a birthday while at school? Celebrate by sending the party to the dorm!

Party hats

Streamers

Birthday banner

Colorful paper straws

Pin the Tail on the Donkey game

Popcorn

iTunes gift card

Playing cards

Gift card to a cupcake shop or bakery for a "birthday cake"

School Spirit!

Send items featuring the school colors or the school mascot. For example, are they the Tigers? Send tiger-print socks.

Gloves or mittens in school colors

Washi tape

Silly String

Coffee mug

Bead necklaces from the party store

Season pass or individual tickets for athletic or theater events on campus

Basket of Sunshine

This is one of my personal favorites. The theme is simple: yellow. Buy anything yellow or package anything in yellow wrapping. It's a simple way to add a little sunshine to your student's day!

Lemon drops

Yellow Silly String

Juicy Fruit gum

Honey straws

Lemonade mix

Sunbutter

Yellow nail polish

Peanut M&M's

Burt's Bees products

Wheat Thins

Sending Our Love and All That Jazz

Our daughter is a music lover with a particular affinity to jazz. This one is especially appreciated if you happen to have a music major. Otherwise, use this as inspiration to send your own care package tailored to your child's major.

"Jazzmin" tea bags

A love "note"

Saxophone reed (or whatever reed or instrument-care item he may use)

A mix CD of favorite jazz tunes

Tickets to an upcoming concert

Hershey's Kisses or foil-heart chocolates

Sheet music

Around the World

Is your student considering a study abroad experience? Try sending a package with international flair. I like to shop at Asian and Hispanic markets for traditional food items or World Market for affordable, unique international items.

Belgian chocolates

German pens

Chinese fortune cookies

French roast coffee

Ramen noodles

Postage stamps

Postcards

Guatemalan worry dolls

Luggage tag

Travel magazine

Gift card to an ethnic restaurant

Vegemite (an Australian "delicacy")

Finals Survival Kit

Get an A+ on this one! Cram (get it—cram?) in some goodies to help your student reduce stress as she prepares for final exams.

Smarties candies

Relaxing herbal tea

Slippers or socks

Lavender hand cream

Shower gel

Brain food (healthier snacks such as nuts, trail mix, dried fruit, popcorn, KIND bars)

Earplugs

Cup of Inspiration

This one is all about things your student can pop in the microwave and drink. Don't forget to slip in some words of inspiration too!

Coffee mug

Hot cocoa

Gourmet teas

Coffee packets

Individual just-add-water soup mixes

Stir sticks made of plastic spoons dipped in chocolate

Flavored coffee creamers

Halloween

The dollar store is a great place to get a bunch of spooktacular treats!

Mini pumpkins

Black Sharpie for drawing on pumpkins

Orange and black socks

Glow-in-the-dark skeleton

Spider rings

Halloween candy

Twelve Days of Christmas

We celebrate Christmas in our house. Our tradition is to give a little individually wrapped gift for the twelve days leading up to Christmas. I number them from one to twelve so she can open one each day.

Gloves/mittens

Candy cane

Book

Gum

Notepad

Lip balm/lip gloss

Chocolates

Travel-sized hand cream

Gift cards (coffee shop, restaurant, store, etc.)

Ticket to a sporting or theater event

Magazine

Flash drive

Holiday Cookie Decorating Kit

This can be tweaked to represent whatever holiday your family celebrates. It's a fun activity for your child and friends.

Unfrosted sugar or shortbread cookies

Shelf-stable frosting(s)

Plastic knives for spreading frosting

Assorted sprinkles and candies

Ziploc bags or plastic containers for storing

Presidential Greetings from Home

On President's Day, send a presidential note and include "pictures" of presidents—in the form of dollar bills.

$1

$5

$10

$20

Be My Valentine

Remember the days of handmade valentines for your friends? Send a valentine-making kit for your student to share with friends.

Crafty items such as glitter, glue, pom-poms, and ribbon

Markers

Card stock

Stickers

Postage stamps

Conversation hearts candy

Saint Paddy's Day: Pot o' Treats

Send anything green! Don't forget to hit the dollar store or party store for some St. Paddy's Day flair.

Pistachios

St. Paddy's hat

Gold-foil-wrapped chocolates (for a pot o' gold)

Green nail polish

Lucky Charms cereal

Junior Mints

Tic Tacs

Spearmint gum

Irish Spring soap (put in a Ziploc bag so it doesn't make the food items taste like soap)

An "Eggstra" Special Spring

Whether you celebrate Easter as a religious holiday or a spring celebration, this care package will be a hit. Along with the items listed below, you can fill a dozen plastic eggs with tiny treats (candies, coins, dollar bills, etc.) and place them in a plastic egg carton.

Peeps

Spring-scented room spray

EOS lip balm (it's in the shape of an egg)

Water bottle

Spring magazine

Jelly beans

Tickets to a spring baseball game

ABOUT THE AUTHOR

Kelly Radi launched her firstborn off to college in 2014 and will send her second out to sea in 2017. A public speaker since 2010, Radi thoroughly enjoys empowering parents as they launch their college-bound students. Radi can be found speaking at high schools and colleges about this emotional transition. She blends her authentic voice with her tell-it-like-it-is approach to offer relevant, practical solutions to help parents (and students) survive—and thrive!—as they set sail.

Radi owns Radi to Write, LLC, a public relations writing firm. Her creative writing appears regularly on various websites and blogs and in regional and national magazines. She lives in Sartell, Minnesota.

Learn more about Kelly Radi at **outtoseaparentsguide.com**.